I0469807

Effective Communication

5 Essential Tips and Exercises to Improve How You Communicate in This Divided World, Even If It Is About Politics, Race or Gender!

Max J. Harrison

accurate, up to date, and reliable, complete information. No warranties of any kind are declared or implied. Readers acknowledge that the author is not engaging in the rendering of legal, financial, medical or professional advice. The content within this book has been derived from various sources. Please consult a licensed professional before attempting any techniques outlined in this book.

By reading this document, the reader agrees that under no circumstances is the author responsible for any losses, direct or indirect, which are incurred as a result of the use of information contained within this document, including, but not limited to, — errors, omissions, or inaccuracies.

Table of Contents

Introduction

Hello there!

How've you been? Exhausted?

It's understandable. Failing to effectively get your point across in communication, particularly in the relationships we have to deal with daily such as family, friends or even co-workers can make you feel drained.

After all, if you have to explain yourself twenty million times, who wouldn't be annoyed, right? Do you hear that little voice inside your head, the one that keeps agreeing with everything you just read—quite the antagonizer isn't it?

It feels an awful lot like you're mad at the people around you, doesn't it? It's as if their misunderstanding and failing to fall in line is a reflection on who they are as people.

Well, be that as it may, have you ever wondered if there is something you could fix in terms of how *you* are communicating?

Think about it—have you been having trouble communicating? Have you ever felt like what you are saying and what you mean aren't really the same, and you haven't been coming across well?

Yes?

Have you ever wondered why?

The lack of dynamic communication at work and home is extremely damaging to both careers and healthy family life. This is because feeling frustrated or unheard when dealing with people you engage with daily is basically the textbook build up to a mental breakdown. As human beings, we need to know that what we do matters, and we need to feel respected and appreciated. And the only way to ensure that, is by working on our communication skills, so we are better equipped to understand and deal with one another.

So, how are you supposed to do all of that? Look no further, here at Effective Communication—5 Essential Tips and Exercises to Improve How You Communicate in This Divided World, Even If It Is About Politics, Race or Gender!—we have you covered!

With modern day communication becoming more and more difficult, with so many divisive issues such as race and religious freedom being pushed to the forefront, it's understandable that people with different views would have a tough time finding common ground from where they can respectfully disagree. But it's not impossible!

And we are here to walk you through exactly how to do this!

Ready?

It's okay; you don't have to be—for now, just listen.

When you are communicating, or when you are being communicated with, there are five key concepts that will determine how effective this communication is going to be. They are often called the five Core Concepts of Communication and are listening, delivery, empathy, honesty, and winning. Every single one of these topics has the unique ability to help change minds and attitudes when properly applied.

You know what that means, right?

It means no more fights at the dinner table or pulling your hair out over what your boss has been saying. Once you've gone through this book and actively applied each of these five techniques, you'll be ready to take on the world—literally!

So, what do you say?

Are you ready now?

Awesome! Keep scrolling; we got you!

Chapter One: Learning to Listen

"The most basic of all human needs is the need to understand and the need to be understood. The best way to understand people is to listen to them." – Ralph Nichols

So, when we think of communication, we, like most other people, tend to look for ways in which we can *impart* knowledge, rather than *take it in*. Think about it. When you are thinking of communication, you really only think about speaking. In fact, even when you *are* thinking about listeners, you think of them in context of speakers, like they exist solely to support speaking.

But that doesn't really make sense, does it? If listeners only have value when there is a speaker, isn't it the same for a speaker? Aren't they also worthless on their own?

And yet, great orators and speakers are lauded and rewarded, whereas listeners are considered to be superfluous to the entire experience.

This is because in modern history, mainly Western history, the emphasis has always been on the individual who commands the crowd. This is why when communicating we believe that the only way to connect is to speak, but in doing so, we are overlooking a key element—our audience.

Who are we speaking to?

What are they doing?

What should they be doing?

Right?

Wrong.

Hold up and rewind for a second. Did you notice that while you were going through this whole passage, you immediately mentally assigned yourself as the speaker and thought of X, Y or Z as the listener? Why do you think that is?

Well, frankly, it's because of power—the concept of being the person in control of a crowd rather than being one of the people who is being controlled makes you feel like you are more authoritative and better than your listener. This brings us to the next issue—respect. Because listeners are deemed to be 'weaker,' you also mentally categorize them to be less worthy of your respect. This in turn totally offsets the communication balance and makes your communication very one-sided.

Let's start by fixing this.

Before you focus on what another person should be doing, or what you think they need to do, why not first focus on building your own communication skills? Before you go off and try to teach other people how to listen to you, why not learn how to listen to others?

Think you're up for the challenge?

Great!

What we're going to learn right now is called Active Listening. Active listening is a technique that attunes you to the speaker so that you are not only focused on the speaker's words but also their body language. This is critical as non-verbal communication can play a crucial role in terms of verifying the authenticity of the information that you are receiving.

The goal of active listening is to ensure that as you are spoken to, you genuinely try to take in the information that is being provided. Think of it like this— if your mom is asking you to get her a sheet of paper so she can note something down while she is on the phone, and you come back with only a sheet of paper, have you actually listened?

What if I said—no?

The key issue in her statement was that she wanted the

sheet of paper so she could take *a note*. Now ask yourself, is a blank sheet of paper going to be useful without a pen or pencil?

You see, listening is about more than words registering in your mind, it's about understanding the intent and purpose conveyed by those words so that *you* can help facilitate a solution based on those cues. There are many techniques you can use to enhance your listening skills. Since you are just beginning, why don't we start with nine necessary steps that can help?

So, are you ready to become a Master Listener?

Awesome!

Here we go!

Technique 1: Offering Support

Have you ever wondered why you feel comfortable saying things to some people and uncomfortable saying things to others? Why do you think that is? Well, it's because some people have indicated to you, either overtly or subliminally that you are safe with them, and that you can confide in them and that you are being taken seriously. Now, if you feel like that when *you* are speaking, and if someone who is just listening can make you feel comfortable or uncomfortable, don't you think you have the ability to do the same when *you*'re the listener?

So, how can you do that?

Scenario One:

Let's say that, you are a professor, and you have an exam to conduct in roughly ten to fifteen minutes. At this time, your colleague who has been having a rough time with management has come to you to speak about the issue because they believe you can help them.

You want to help them, and you want to hear them out, but you're looking at the hall clock every two minutes and are slowly inching toward the classroom as you nod distractedly to their tirade.

How do you think your colleague feels?

Do you think they feel heard?

The odds are they don't, and that's understandable. You would feel the same.

Well, let's go back and evaluate what went wrong. When your colleague came to talk to you, you knew two things. (a) That you have a class in ten minutes, and (b) that they wished to converse with you on a topic that was going to take more than ten minutes. The problem was that both of these issues are incompatible, which means that by saying nothing, you are putting yourself in an impossible position. Not only are you not going to get to class on time at this rate, you also won't be able to make your colleague feel like you valued their time or shared their concern. In short, they will have felt cut off and unsupported.

What you just did was "passive" listening. Your role as a listener was inert and did not respond to the circumstances. So, what would "active" listening look like in this case?

Well, to begin—active listening assesses.

So, when your colleague came to discuss the problem, as an active listener, you would've realized you didn't have enough time to finish the conversation right now.

So, if you had told your colleague you had a class in ten minutes and as this was an important issue that would take longer than the ten minutes you could spare now, you would have expressed that although you wish to help them, you can't at this moment.

Then, for good measure, if you added a suitable time when you are free, you'd be actually putting in a concentrated effort. Not only would you be telling them that they matter, verbally, but you would be using an action to follow up that behavior.

Now, you can get to class on time, *and* your colleague doesn't think you're a prat! Win-win!

Technique 2: Creating Openings

So, have you ever felt claustrophobic?

You know, when you feel everything was closing in on you? When there was just too much pressure bearing down on you, and you needed to get up and be able to get away? Well, that is another common side effect of bad communication.

You see, communication needs to be liberating. When you as a listener, aren't making your speaker feel safe and secure, your speaker will have a harder time explaining what the problem is and will be more inclined to lie or to put on an act.

With good communication, you can make your speaker

feel like there is a large berth between the two of you, not one that keeps you away from them, but one that gives them room to breathe, and not feel like they are being interrogated by the Spanish Inquisition.

Basically, you need to encourage them to speak, but you also need to enable them to make a choice. So, give them an opening, but don't grab 'em by the collar.

Let's give things a little context, shall we?

Scenario Two:

Your boyfriend, Clark has had a rough day. He used to be a high flyer with a great job, but after this new company called Stark Enterprises moved in, he lost his job. He has been unemployed for months, and this evening upon coming home from work, you notice that the house is a mess and he has red-rimmed eyes.

Which of the following should be your response?

Response 1: Clark, what's wrong? Are you upset about the job?

Response 2: Hey Babe, it's been a rough day hasn't it? Shit happens; you'll get better opportunities.

Response 3: Hey Babe, the house is nuts. Why don't we get dressed and grab dinner outside, and we can deal with this stuff later?

Response 4: Hey you, are you okay?

In Response one you are basically cornering your boyfriend. Clark now feels very much like you've put him on the spot and is automatically going into a defensive mode where he is feeling like an underperformer because you mentioned his lost job. He has to pretend otherwise because you already suspected that the behavior could be due to his loss of a job.

You won't get anywhere with that, and in instances like Response two, where you steamroll through his answer, don't really help either. So, what should you do?

Response three ignored the entire premise and tries to change the topic to something lighter like dinner plans. The problem with that though, is now Clark feels like his troubles aren't important enough to merit a conversation, and you can't be bothered to talk about it which is why you are both mentally and physically avoiding the issue.

The ideal response is Response four, where you have shown a good amount of interest and indicated that you are open to a conversation should Clark wish to have one. But you have not been specific enough to let on that you know something is wrong, giving Clark control to now either tell you or avoid the issue.

Pretty cool, eh?

Technique 3: Mirror, Mirror

Another technique that you'll want to master is the Mirror technique or as it is commonly known, the Reflection technique. When dealing with a distraught speaker, it is important to reinforce what the speaker is saying. Because you are the listener and you want to allow the speaker to guide the conversation, the best way to reinforce is to reflect instead of adding in opinions.

For instance, if you are dealing with someone who perhaps is saying, "I am upset," you shouldn't use a strong reinforcement by saying, "Yes, you're very upset." This would serve no purpose. However, if you instead reflected the person's statement either by rephrasing or by turning it into a light question, such as, "Oh dear, are you?" or "You're upset?" What you are doing is prompting the speaker to keep going. By zeroing in on the key term and reflecting it to them as a mirror would, you're sending the ball back into their court, and they can explain what is going on and why, without you trying to guess.

Reflection is a crucial technique to use when dealing with individuals of the opposite gender—remember that saying, *Women are from Venus, and Men are from Mars.* Do you know why people say that? It's because different genders often have different reactions to things. The reflection method allows you to ensure that the speaker is the one who is telling the story, so there is no room for assumptions, which makes it a great gender contextualization tool.

Scenario Three:

Let's say that you, Mark, are dealing with your female best friend, Casey in the middle of a meltdown. You and Casey have five common friends and Hazel is one of them.

Casey: I am so mad right now. That trip was a disaster.

Mark: You're upset?

Casey: Yes! I'd been planning this vacation for ages, and Hazel totally ruined it!

Mark: You thought it was going to be a great trip.

Casey: I did. I put a lot of effort into it and planned for three months. I was really looking forward to it!

Now, when you start to listen to Casey, you start by thinking that this entire tirade is about Hazel, who supposedly ruined the trip. Your instinct would be to focus on Hazel, and wonder what did Hazel do, right?

But here is the thing. Hazel wasn't the most important part of the conversation. What she's really doing is expressing how upset she is, and that is precisely why, when you focus on that, by reflecting her emotions back to her, by focusing on what she was feeling, as opposed to who she was venting about, you are allowing her to center herself.

Remember the point of reflection is for you to help the speaker focus on what they want to say and stay on track, using soft surface level questions initially. Then as the conversation deepens focus on circumstances, so you show that you do understand the main issue they are trying to explain.

See! Women aren't so different after all!

Technique 4: Reading between the Lines

Another technique that works really well, particularly when it comes to dealing with children and customers (if you work in sales or deal with customers or clients daily) is reading between the lines. This is a great technique to combine with Reflection, as it helps balance the flow of the conversation which is super important when you are dealing with children.

The key to this technique is your voice. Since there is a bit of guesswork involved here, and in addition to reflecting, you'll also be trying to guess what is going on, it is important that your voice is very soft and moldable as if you are suggesting a possible thought, as opposed to making a hard decision.

Let's start with an example.

Scenario Four:

Your child, Kevin comes home from school visibly upset and is unwilling to talk about it. You suspect that Kevin may be the victim of bullying, and you want to start a discussion on the topic.

Parent: Kevin, hey buddy, you want to tell me what's up?

Kevin: Nothing's up. I'm fine.

Parent: You look like you may be a little disturbed. Did you have a bad day at school?

Kevin: Why do you care? It's not like you even know what's going on in my life!

Parent: I do care Kevin, and I would like to know what's going on because I'm concerned. Did someone say or do something to you?

Kevin: You don't have to be. No one said anything new.

Parent: Have people been saying things for a while now? What have they been saying?

Kevin: That I'm stupid. I failed all my AP classes.

Parent: Wow, that's a really harsh thing to say. Who's been saying this to you?

Kevin: Donny Sanderson and Mickey Ports.

Parent: When did this begin?

.... (conversation continues)

The key to reading between the lines is to stay on track no matter what. You'll notice that throughout this entire conversation, Kevin tries to distract his parent multiple times. Initially, he tried denial which didn't work because the parent follows up with a specific question, forcing Kevin to address the issue. As he is unwilling to do so, he then tries to piss them off so that they would back off in anger. But the parent refuses to be lead on, taking a quick minute to reinforce that they do indeed care deeply for him. They move on to what they believe is the crux of the matter.

It is at this point that Kevin starts to open up. He leaves an open-ended statement which the parent follows up by asking what has been going on, and how long it's been happening. At this point, Kevin tries one more time to distract the parent by telling them the cause, and then another thing that he feels the parent will react to—he's failing all his AP classes. The parent has to be careful to follow up on what is essential at that moment so that the conversation keeps flowing, and you'll note that's exactly what happens, and voila, now Kevin is finally feeling secure enough to open up and talk.

Technique 5: Clarifying

So, have you ever felt like you were talking at cross purposes or what someone is saying, and what you are understanding are two different things? Yeah? Well, here's the quick fix for that. What you are dealing with here is a lack of clear communication and the best way to fix that issue as a responsible listener is to clarify.

Now, we understand that stopping someone mid-tirade may seem difficult, but it is a key element in ensuring that you know exactly what is going on. What's more, when you are clarifying, you are also forcing the speaker to acknowledge what they are saying, and often, they can hear their own absurdity! This is perfect for the difficult Thanksgiving when you have the Trump-supporting uncle going on a tirade against immigrants taking American jobs, and you really want to engage in a heated debate but need to hear him out first.

Keep in mind, that it is essential to let a person finish speaking no matter how badly you may want to interrupt them with a piece of your mind because allowing them to complete their thoughts shows respect towards the speaker. If you aren't respecting the speaker, the speaker won't respect you!

Why don't we show you how to go about this "clarifying" business?

Scenario Five:

At Thanksgiving, as you are sitting around the table, your Trump-loving Uncle Drumpf is having a fit about how people aren't appreciating all the good things that Ol' Donny is doing for the country and is ranting about how immigrants are ruining America by stealing American jobs.

Uncle Drumpf: The American public needs to wake up and smell the coffee. Mr. Trump is the best president we've had in decades. He's making America great again.

You: Oh! That's an interesting viewpoint—how do you think he is making America great again?

Uncle Drumpf: Well, he's doing it all. He's running the country, and the economy is booming. We ain't got Mexicans or immigrants coming in no more.

You: How is the economy booming, Uncle?

Uncle Drumpf: We got more jobs and stuff in his first year than we did in Obama's last.

You: I see. What about this issue with immigrants? Why do you dislike them?

Uncle Drumpf: Cause they're not from here. They're immigrants!

You: So, you dislike them because they are not originally from America, but have moved here?

Uncle Drumpf: Well, no, not really. It's just that they keep stealing our jobs!

You: They're stealing our jobs?

Uncle Drumpf: Hell yeah! Down at the factory, there are hundreds of us white folk who ain't getting jobs, but they keep bringing in more "skilled-labor," and then they take our jobs.

You: Do you think then that only white Americans are American?

Uncle Drumpf: I didn't say that! Don't play the race card!

You: Okay, so what do you think "skilled labor" is?

Uncle Drumpf: It's when they let in people who are trained to do certain things.

.... (conversation continues)

Now a lot is going on here with the whole discussion. On the one hand, you have a slightly antagonistic Uncle you're trying to keep in line, and on the other, you're also trying to control yourself because with every sentence out of his mouth you are dying to go on a tirade against him.

Here is the problem, though. Yelling at each other till you're both blue in the face won't solve anything. That's why in courts when one side speaks the other side stays silent, and while the other side speaks the first side stays silent. It's symbiotic.

Does that mean you should passively listen and hopefully, tune him out so that you don't have to listen to his racist views? Well, no, because that doesn't help either—if you aren't listening to him, how are you going to figure out why he thinks the way he does. What is driving him? Does he have misconceptions? What are they?

This is where you come in with the questions. Clarification questions not only show that you are listening, but they also underpin a conversation so that when you want to go back and address these issues, you know what to say. This allows you and the speaker to be able to move towards finding more common ground and is great for conflict resolution.

Technique 6: Supportive Silences

Interestingly enough, all of this doesn't mean that whenever you are listening to someone you need to actively speak or engage to show that you are invested in the conversation. Silences have a way of being extremely engaging, especially if you are close enough to a person. That's why you'll notice you don't mind the silence with people you are comfortable with, whereas silences when you're with a new crowd can make you feel uncomfortable or like you need to do something or say something.

Ideally, you can manipulate silences so that they seem supportive and so your speaker realizes you want more information and can provide accordingly. This is super important because while clarification and reflection can on occasion sound really fake, you don't have to worry about that with silence as your body language and nonverbal cues are speaking for you.

Let's look at two contrasting examples.

Scenario Six:

Your friend, Nayeem was the victim of an atrocious shooting attack at his mosque when he went to pray. He lost his younger brother, Abrar in the shooting and has only just returned to school after a week of grieving. He is now staring outside the window. Noticing that he is alone, you come up to speak to him, and the conversation goes as follows:

You: Hey man, I heard what happened—I'm really sorry for your loss. It must be hard. (You are sitting quietly at his side, your face showing concern and distress, but you remain otherwise silent, waiting to see if he wants to respond)

Nayeem: It's just so senseless; he was just four years old.

You: It's hard to make sense of brutality like that.

Nayeem: He had his whole life ahead of him. Why would someone do that to a child? How is that fair?

You: It's not.

Nayeem: I just hope people learn from this. Terrorism comes in all shapes and forms, but the sense of loss is always the same. I miss him so much.

Here your silence combined with your soft reflections has allowed your friend, Nayeem to speak up. If instead, you had been uncomfortable with the silence, you would be trying to draw parallels, or add more information—and Nayeem's final revelation when he realizes that more than anything else, he just misses his baby brother, would not have happened. This is bad because you have not helped Nayeem do anything. You are taking away from his moment of pain by talking about similar incidents or other people who have been through things, whereas all Nayeem really needed was to come to terms with how he felt and why he felt that way.

Always keep in mind though, that silence needs to be using sparingly. If you're always all quiet while you are listening you will come off as a passive listener who isn't invested.

Technique 7: Summarization

Now let's move on to one of our favorites—summarization.

Why is this a favorite?

Ever had a bad boss? Like a really terrible boss who would say he told you to do A, B, and C but in truth, he only told you to do A, and now you are being blamed for his incompetence? How about difficult parents who would assign you tasks and then come back and say you missed X, Y, and Z.

The best way to deal with these situations is to use the summarization technique.

So, the way this technique works is by using a three-step process:

First, the information is imparted by the speaker, who tells the listener what needs to be done. Secondly, the information given is repeated by the listener in their own words to check with the speaker and ensure that they have correctly understood what tasks they have been assigned. The third step is a byproduct. Here the actions are being publicly announced, as you repeat them, so there is little room to misunderstand.

Let's run through a basic example.

Scenario Seven:

You are a teacher and have been working with a particularly difficult child, Paul. Paul is usually a good kid, but he hates studying, so he always makes excuses and claims that he wasn't aware of the extra coursework that was set, or of the homework assigned. His behavior is now becoming problematic because he is falling behind in class. A great way to provide an instant check on Paul's behavior is to use the Summarization technique.

Teacher: You've missed your homework for all of your classes this week and three of your coursework assignments as well. If you really want to stay in the same class with your friends, you will have to submit all of those by the end of next week and make sure the rest of your assignments this year are on time and are graded C or above.

Paul: I want to stay with my friends.

Teacher: Why don't you go through what you need to do, then. Maybe it'll help you remember.

Paul: I need to submit all of my missed homework and coursework assignments by the end of this week. That's Friday, right?

Teacher: That's right, what else?

Paul: I need to maintain a minimum of a C in all of my other assignments this year and send them in on time

Teacher: Well done, yes!

Now, by encouraging Paul to be an active listener instead of a passive one, you have ensured that he has repeated and gone through the issues you mentioned. Now, not only has he heard it, he doesn't get to say he didn't hear you or that he missed that bit about the minimum C you told him to maintain. This helps not only clarify understanding but also to chart progress later on.

Technique 8: Contextualization

A super important part of any conversation is context. You see, when a speaker is speaking they control the narrative, and as such, they deliberately include or leave out the bits of the story that are beneficial or detrimental to them. Now, this can happen due to a multitude of reasons. It could be that the speaker has merely not noticed the importance of the incidents they chose to avoid, or they could feel that those incidents take away from the core issue.

This is why listening is so important, particularly in the world of alternative facts. Focusing on what is being said and taking in the information helps prevent superficial reactions such as broad generalizations or snapshot information. It is important to instead keep in mind that all information is always contextual. Which means that when and if you are dealing with a speaker who is forming their version of a story, it is important to use context-based questions to challenge and draw out the full story.

Scenario Eight:

In the given scenario, we are dealing with a Sandy Hook truther, (an individual who does not believe that the Sandy Hook massacre was real and instead believes that crisis actors were used to stage an event that could adversely impact gun control laws) influenced by Infowars and Alex Jones. By using contextualized questions, you can force your speaker to identify inconsistencies with their own narrative, and this helps immensely when dealing with individuals who have drastically different takes on issues. Note the following:

SH Truther: The whole Sandy Hook thing was a scam; nobody's taking my guns with that stuff.

You: Why do you think it was a scam?

SH Truther: Alex Jones did a whole report that explained it all.

You: Is Alex Jones a dependable source?

SH Truther: He has his own show, and Mr. Trump endorses him.

You: Haven't they both been called out for using and promoting fake news? How do you know they are telling the truth?

SH Truther: If he wasn't telling the truth the government would have stopped him.

You: Well, actually Alex Jones is being sued for defamation, and he's already lost three suits, meaning the courts are declaring him guilty of spreading propaganda.

When you start to put things in context and force the speaker to do so as well, you'll find that you can both streamline discussions and deal with deliberate attempts to fit facts to a narrative by forcing the speaker to acknowledge the narrative. This is super helpful when dealing with confrontational people who don't like to or want to admit that they are wrong.

In this example, your first question seeks to draw information. The speaker is convinced that the issue was a scam, then you force him to explain why they believe so, and what their sources are, etc. Your second question challenges their sources which forces them to back it up, which is again challenged in your follow-up question. They then try to use logic to defend the situation, which is answered by your final point where you show him that the assumptions he had based his narrative on were incorrect.

Contextualization is very important because if someone comes up to you and says X, Y, or Z called you a bad name, instead of lashing out, you need first to understand the context. Understanding or seeking context does not mean you are against them or saying they are wrong. It merely means that to fully comprehend a situation you need all of the information, not just the information they want you to have to fuel their side of the story—that's how alternative facts are born.

Technique 9: Rinse and Repeat

And this brings us to our final technique—repetition.

It's important for you to keep in mind that human beings are slaves of habit, and that means all of the habits you have developed didn't just pop up one fine morning. They developed over years and years of positive behavior. What do we mean?

Do you know the story of Pavlov and his dog?

No?

Well, a Russian psychologist called Ivan Pavlov, came up with this thing called classical conditioning. Every day, he would ring a bell and within five to ten seconds he would place a big, juicy steak out for his dog to eat. A few weeks later he replaced the steak with minced meat, and a few weeks after that he used meat powder. Finally, he stopped putting anything out at all, and yet the one thing that wouldn't change was the dog's reaction. The second he heard the bell he would start salivating in anticipation. It's because he was trained to think in this way.

Why is this important?

Because the same goes for humans. With active listening, you can actually train yourself to think in a specific manner and do the same to your speakers. For instance, if your speaker notices that you pay enough attention to engage in contextualized questions, you'll find they steer away from propaganda-inspired generalizations because they don't want to feel embarrassed like they did the first time.

It's a learned reaction. You have to keep consciously telling yourself to do better, or to summarize, or reflect, or even to use supportive silence, and at some point, you'll find that you can do all of that instinctively because you have trained your brain to react in that way.

Who says, you can't teach an "old dog" new tricks?

Here is an example.

Scenario Nine:

You have been dealing with five managers who have had difficulties processing problems from their teams. To help increase their ability to listen to problems actively, the managers were given a question and answer sheet every time they had to deal with a problematic employee. There was a checklist provided which encouraged the managers to get to the root of the problems by asking a series of questions. One year later, upper management found that the difficulties originally being processed were no longer an issue, and the checklist sheet wasn't even necessary because the managers were asking the relevant questions themselves.

The continuous repetition of the process led to the principles of active listening becoming embedded in the managers—a perfect example of rinse and repeat.

Check Yourself

Learning techniques to help you improve your listening skills is a commendable thing to do. But before you move on, you really need to take an in depth look at what you want to achieve. Why are you looking to improve your listening skills? What are the complaints you have received? What are the losses in terms of the relationships that you have sustained?

Be honest; be brutally honest.

Learning how to listen all over again after years of not listening isn't going to be easy, and this, right here, is your motivation. It's what's going to keep you going every time you slip up.

Take a minute, or take ten—but figure out what matters to you. Remember always look at the bigger picture.

To-Do Drills—Your OFFICIAL Action Items

Okay, so we're done with all the heavy lifting but how do we make sure you can put all these techniques to use?

First, take a little mental break—you just learned a bunch of stuff, and your brain is in overdrive grab a glass of water (stay hydrated!) and then before you keep reading do a mental recap of the stuff you just learned.

All done?

Great, now while these tips are important for your understanding of active listening and how it works, you also need to have an easy way to implement them. Let's start by checking to see if you are doing these five things.

1. Are you maintaining eye contact?

We know we haven't really emphasized it, but it's really a given. Eye contact is a critical part of any form of communication. But it's especially important when it comes to listening since it is one of the few actual actions you are engaging in. Eye contact helps to ensure balance and makes sure your speaker is feeling heard while you are also staying focused.

2. Are you keeping an open mind?

This is particularly important in today's political climate. Look, we get that you may not agree with or even like a lot of the political conversations going on, but what about the people? You don't have to like them, but do you care about them? If your answer is yes, you *need* to find a way to try to understand where they are coming from. You don't need to agree with them; you don't even need to see eye to eye, but by at least understanding how they think, you are creating room to have a dialogue. In the end, it's not fist fighting, but conversations that change the world.

3. Don't interrupt and don't be a Problem-solver!

You're not a plumber, and even if you are, you're not a conversational plumber. Your job isn't to go over to see what's wrong and put things right—it's to listen and try to understand. Interrupting ensures you are never going to understand because it means you are listening to respond and not to understand. The same goes for offering solutions. Get off your high horse. This isn't what listening is about.

4. Are you waiting before you ask for clarification?

Yes, we know we said clarification is a crucial part of the listening process, but that doesn't mean you should be asking for clarification all the time. There is a time and place for everything. You don't ask for an explanation in the middle of a sentence. Hold your horses; it's like traffic. You can speak when the red light goes on, and the speaker takes a break, and even so, phrase it nicely so that it shows you are asking because you want to know, not to challenge them.

5. Are you keeping up with the Non-Verbal cues?

Outside of the realm of chat lines and emails, much of the communication we have is non-verbal. Your tone, or your facial expression, or even the way you are holding yourself all mean something and are critical to the proper assessment of a situation. Enter active listening. Remember, active listeners assess, and the best way to do so is to identify what your speaker feels so you can cater for that issue.

See, that wasn't really that hard, now was it?

The next time you are listening to someone, keep these five tips in mind. Why don't you make a note of how much better the experience is for both of you!

Chapter Two: How to Make People Want to Listen

"Great communication depends on two simple skills—Context, which attunes a leader to the same frequency as his or her audience, and Delivery which allows a leader to phrase messages in a language the audience can understand."—John C. Maxwell

While being a good listener is a critical component of any act of communication, the most important thing that you will be dealing with when you try to practice effective communication is speaking.

But here's the catch. It's not really the words that you are using that are the most important thing; your words or language skills are a modem. They are the manner through which you are engaging, but what you really need to work on is your delivery. You see, that is about skill, and believe it or not it can be developed.

Now, we are going to go into the basics of effective delivery and its cornerstones. But first, we are going to take a quick detour to highlight what we mean by effective communication. Why now?

Because in the first chapter, you were dealing with listening, and listening, while an important component of communication, doesn't require as much activity as the actual delivery process. Now, without further ado, let's get going.

Understanding Effective Communication

Effective communication is generally a business term, and it's something that is generally used to ensure that a complete, coherent form of communication is being undertaken, and in such a manner that the person you are communicating with understands the message conveyed in the way in which the communicator intended it to be understood.

Pretty easy, right?

What you just did is the single most complicated thing mankind has ever done. In fact, only the human race is capable of full communication, to the extent of ensuring that the message we deliver is "conveyed in the manner in which the communicator intended it to be understood."

Generally, we turn to the seven C's of communication.

Correctness, whereby you ensure that the information you are delivering is correct and accurate. *Clarity* makes sure you aren't complicating things, remember to stay focused and stick to one issue. The best way to do that is to ensure you are *Concise*, cover what needs to be covered without embellishment, don't create too much build up just get in there, and get to the point. Having said that, it is equally important that you keep an eye out to ensure that the message being sent is *Complete*. And then in quick succession, you have *Consideration, Concreteness,* and *Courtesy.* To ensure that you are being kind and considerate, we'll cover consideration more thoroughly in chapter three when we talk about empathy. Your concreteness comes from the authenticity of what you are saying, and to finish off, there is a courtesy which is the polish on top that keeps the audience happy and willing to listen.

But all of this is about the message we are dealing with— how we *deliver* this message is a whole other issue.

So, let's get straight to it, shall we?

How to Deliver Effectively

When you are delivering any form of communication, whether in person or over a telephone call there are common factors that help ensure that the delivery of the topic is top-notch. Now, not all of these methods apply to all forms of delivery, and that is okay. You don't need to cover all of these issues at the same time every time you speak. Try to address as many of the issues as you can positively, and you'll find that, not only has your delivery improved drastically, but so has your self-confidence.

Ready?

1. Posture

When you are face to face with whoever you are speaking to, your body language or your posture plays a significant role in how they perceive whatever you say. One of the best ways to ensure that you seem strong and confident on stage is to create a solid stance. You'll notice that when newscasters or professional speakers are talking, they don't sway or rock. They almost invariably have a strong, stable stance that allows them to maintain secure footing. The best way to do this is to ensure that your feet are spread to the same width as your shoulders so that the four corners of your body now create some sort of balance. That allows you to look more grounded and confident.

You can replicate a similar posture even if you are sitting down, by placing your feet flat on the floor, and exerting a bit of upward pressure so that you are sitting up straight and tall, and have clear airways and lungs with which to speak.

What we are doing now is called confident posture. By pulling our shoulders back and keeping our arms and legs either relaxed or in a strong stance, we are expressing assertiveness, telling our audience that we know what we are doing and that they are in safe hands.

While confident posturing is great for meetings and presentations, if you are dealing with something more personal you want to try to establish open posturing. This is particularly important when you are dealing with friends and family. In an open posture, keep your hands apart and your legs apart when standing. Often, the hands are kept face up to show vulnerability, and to help show that you are willing and open to communication.

Say you are having an intense discussion with your Aunt Macy. Aunt Macy is a wonderful woman who bakes amazing southern biscuits with gravy to die for, but she has one tiny little problem. Aunty Macy loves her guns, and she is a certifiable gun nut.

Aunt Macy takes particular offense to the notion that her First Amendment right could be threatened by the school shootings that have been happening and claims that these are all a ruse to take away her guns. You are trying to have a conversation with her about this but her arms and legs are crossed strongly, and she refuses to listen or be reasoned with.

In the given example, Aunt Macy is depicting a Closed Posture where she is unwilling and openly hostile to the topic. This tells you that now is probably not the best time to discuss the issue with her; she's not open to conversation. However, if you feel that it is imperative that such a conversation happen right away, what you can do is try to distract her, and then come back. The idea being that by the time you start talking about the topic again she'll be in a more open mindset, which you'll be able to judge by taking a quick look at her posture. So, not only does posture allow you to portray a specific image, it also helps you understand what your audience is thinking, which puts you in a better place to be able to judge what information you should be imparting. Crazy isn't it?

2. Voice

Vocal intonation is perhaps the single most powerful weapon afforded to any speaker. A number of different things can determine intonation, including the register used to speak. Generally, studies have shown that a lower register is preferred as people find people who speak from a lower register to be more honest and dependable. Timbre and pitch are also important here because they also contribute to the audience's sense of positivity. Warmer, richer tones are considered to be preferable, which is why politicians train themselves to use low, warm voices when speaking.

Let's say you are a small startup company that is seeking to encourage local people to shop from local farmers as opposed to large supermarkets. Your company works acts as a middle man between the local farmers and the locals. Your company's main objective is customer service, as local farmers can't always provide supplies in bulk, or even necessarily as consistently as supermarkets. When a product is unavailable or for some reason can't be provided, it is your company's job to make sure you can let the consumer down gently.

Do you think it's possible to let someone down gently without upsetting them? Does your tone of voice have anything to do with it?

Well, studies, say that they do!

Casual tones which tend to be more light or airy have proven to upset consumers who are being denied a request, as they perceive it as not being serious. In contrast, a deeper more formal tone is seen as more authoritative and is better received by agitated customers.

3. Eyes

Your second most important weapon when you are dealing with communication is eye contact. The French novelist, Victor Hugo, once suggested that when a woman is speaking we should listen to what she is saying with our eyes as it is where so much of the original communication is taking place. In fact, this is considered to be such a common happenstance that there are numerous phrases which deal with eye-contact or the communication of the eyes, including "keep your eyes open," "a sight for sore eyes," or "apple of one's eyes."

There are four key factors that are expressed by eye contact. The first is intimacy or closeness. This is why when one feels romantically attached to someone else, they tend to increase how long they look at them directly, and this, in turn, is used to understand how close one feels to another. Another key factor is control—eye contact can be used to evaluate how in control of a situation one is. This is why passive dogs tend to blink or look away more, and aggressive, more authoritative dogs will look straight at you. Eye contact can be used to take control of and redirect a conversation, whereas it can also be telling us important stuff like how vital a piece of information is or how credible it is.

That's not all, though. There are specific rules for eye contact. For instance, in a formal situation, your eye contact should be restricted to the other party's eyes only, while in social settings the acceptable area goes down to the bridge of the nose. It is only in intimate settings that looking from one's eyes to their lips is considered acceptable.

In fact, there are ten major factors which affect the human gaze and which your audience will be subconsciously monitoring you on. The first is physical distance. When in very close proximity people tend not to face each other and stare straight at them as it increases awkwardness. However, at a distance constant eye contact is fine. Eye contact also tends to be avoided when the topic of conversation is personal or private, whereas when dealing with conversations regarding opinions more eye contact is common. The same goes for attention-seeking behaviors. Introverts tend to hold a gaze for shorter times than extroverts do making personality traits also indicative of the type of eye contact you are likely to have. Whereas interpersonal skills, cooperation, and attention all seem to demand more eye contact as does physical attractiveness. Finally, individuals with mental illness or with different ethnic backgrounds tend to have different levels of eye contact.

4. Hands

Believe it or not, another part of your body that has way more to say than you actually realize is your hands. Interestingly, most speakers don't even realize that they are moving their hands when they're speaking. This is because it's practically an automatic reaction. That's why so many cultures incorporate hand gestures as a form of greeting. For instance, the folded palms in India when they say "*Namaste,*" in most Muslim cultures the right hand is cupped slightly and brought to the forehead as they say "*Assalamualaikum,*" the generic hand wave as we say "*Hello,*" and even the handshake we use when we meet someone for the very first time.

Every hand gesture communicates a message to the

audience. Why don't we run you through a few examples?

Hidden Hands

Hidden hands have a very negative connotation because the use of hands is considered to be such a basic and common form of communication. When a speaker consciously chooses to remove their hands from view, this is considered to be suspect. They come off unsure and as if they have something to hide.

Palms Up

The reverse is true when dealing with upturned palms which are traditionally mean that the speaker is open and honest, so much so that they are willing to show vulnerability. This, however, is not the same when you have your palms down. Downward palms are a reference to power.

Here the speaker is showing that they are authoritative and dominant; there is no room for debate, and a decision has been made. When the speaker tends to have his palms down they can also come across as aggressive, and as such, this posture should not be maintained for extended periods when dealing with a crowd.

Pointers Out

Have you ever fought with your significant other and had them point their finger at you, literally? Remember how mad it made you? Well, do you want to know why? Pointing fingers is a super aggressive gesture that is considered culturally inappropriate in a multitude of countries including the Philippines and Bangladesh. Multiple studies including that of Pease (2004) discuss the impact that intimidating behavior has on a crowd and advocates against it.

Hand Clasp

Clasped hands or hands that are held together tend to reflective some kind of inner turmoil. The idea is that the clasped hands are preventing the speaker from some sort of negative outburst. Studies on the matter have shown that the more intense the negative tension, the higher the clasped hands tend to be placed. Male speakers tend to use the handclasp to cover their crotch when sitting, as this helps to give a form of mental protection to what they consider to be their most valuable and vulnerable part of the body.

The Steeple

Interestingly, although steepling is quite similar to clasping our hands together, it has a nearly opposite meaning. Politicians are often seen to steeple their hands. This is because the act conveys confidence and focus. Barack Obama, the forty-fourth President of the United States was commonly seen to steeple his hands, particularly during interviews.

Behind the Back

Standing with one's hands behind their back is another common gesture used to portray courage, the exposure of one's chest as a vulnerable part of the body displays confidence, particularly when the hands are clasped behind the back. If however, the hands are not clasped but gripping the elbow or wrist this now portrays nervousness or unsureness.

Hands to Face

The hands to the face on the other hand show anxiousness. Stressed speakers tend to continuously touch their face or hair and tend to attempt to cradle their face or head as you would a baby's. This is definitely the kind of behavior you want to avoid if you are dealing with an audience.

Doctors and nurses, in particular seem to avoid this type of behavior in earnest as they don't have the time to allow the patient to feel anything but confident.

The Neck Touch

The neck touch is an extension of the hand to face tendency although this does project more anxiety than the former.

5. Environment

Your surroundings as you speak are also an important element of any form of communication. Giving a speech at a train station where your speech is muffled by the noise of trains coming and going is unlikely to help your speech have more impact. Alternatively, if you give a speech on a podium with great acoustics and no background noise, the impact of your delivery is more likely to be better received.

6. Face

The Face is considered to be the single most common way to evaluate not only what a person means by what they are saying, but more importantly what they mean in terms of how they feel. This is particularly important as the human face is known to mirror the six universal emotions—happiness, sorrow, surprise, fear, disgust, and rage.

Let's start by focusing on smiling. Smiling faces tend to denote happiness or joy. The human mind can even distinguish between a fake and a real smile. There are a few slight physical differences. With a real smile, the corners of the mouth roll upward, narrowing the eyes in an automatic reaction. This is different from a false smile or the "social smile" which is strained and controlled by the individual.

Almost all human beings deal with things called micro-expressions. Microexpressions are like the tiny details in a book. When read together they can lead to the person in question being influenced to act in a certain way. For instance, there are four microexpressions of the lips other than a simple smile:

1. *The Upside-Down Smile*—The reverse frown is the most common facial expression you'll come across and is indicative of some sort of negative reaction to a specific stimulus, which is either showcasing some form of stress or alternatively saying no to a specific thing.

2. *The Lip Fold*—The lip fold or the purse is also a common facial expression. This in particular deals with contradictory feelings. For instance, if you are telling people that the only way to get to New York from Washington D.C. is by train, and I know that you can

also take a flight or hop on a Greyhound. Even if I don't overtly correct you, the fact that I know that you are imparting flawed knowledge will cause me to silently fold my lips in disapproval. The lip fold is therefore generally used to indicate some sort of negative emotion such as sorrow, unhappiness or distrust, although it seems to be a pretty regular member of the modeling world nowadays as well.

3. The Sneer—Unlike pursed lips, the upward lip curl or the sneer doesn't have alternative meanings. This indicates some version of contempt which like the eye roll is almost universal in its disrespect and disgust. The sneer is most common when and where a total lack of respect has taken place between the two parties and can be a clear indicator of couples who have not been doing well and who are prone to break ups.

4. The Peeking Tongue—When someone is extremely busy or concentrating on something, they are also likely to make short displays of the tongue. The same is also done to show disgust or playfulness but with different facial constructions.

But one's lips form a specific part of their facial reactions. Alternative reactions include the furrowing of the forehead which can indicate concern due to extreme worry or anger. Anger can be seen in the flaring of nostrils, and noses are also crinkled in disgust or repulsion in many cultures similar to the furrowing of brows. And finally, there is blushing which is when the rush of blood to the face causes the face to turn red with either shock or shame, or any other form of stress.

7. Pace

How fast you are speaking can also help control your delivery, with speed being indicative of excitement or stress. When you choose to slow down your delivery, you are forcing the audience to slow down also and to fully take in the information being provided in a slower manner.

8. Prosody

Prosody can also be a very beneficial delivery technique. It refers to the sing-song quality of some speeches which is often attained by using repetitive words to create a flow or a rhythm. IN Martin Luther King Jr's famous speech, he used the phrase " I have a dream" continuously to create a sort of symmetry that gave the dream more force—"I have a dream that one day this nation will rise up and live out the true meaning of its creed: *"We hold these truths to be self-evident; that all men are created equal.*

I have a dream that one day on the red hills of Georgia the sons of former slaves and the sons of former slave owners will be able to sit down together at the table of brotherhood.

I have a dream that one day even the state of Mississippi, a state sweltering with the heat of injustice, sweltering with the heat of oppression, will be transformed into an oasis of freedom and justice.

I have a dream that my four little children will one day live in a nation where they will not be judged by the color of their skin but by the content of their character.

I have a dream today."

The natural rhythm that is being developed not only makes the speech sound better but it makes it catchier and holds attention.

9. Silence

Silence can also play a big role in delivery as well. When properly utilized, being able to use silence to create drama or to force the audience to think results in engagement and the more engaged a person is, the more effective your delivery is!

It can also, however, be a little risky particularly when you are attempting cross-gender communication!

This is generally because men, unlike women, tend to process information silently in their heads, while women tend to lean towards "*talking things out.*" What makes this even worse is that for women, silence is more of an indicator of pain or rage which is why when they see it in men they tend to go on the defensive.

For instance, imagine you are a woman, and you and your boyfriend are having a fight about how often he completes the chores.

You: You never do anything, not even the bed!

Him: What's the point; you get into bed again anyway!

You: That is ridiculous logic. You just want to avoid working!

Him: Well, I don't see what's so wrong with that, to be honest.

You: It's wrong cause the more chores you avoid, the more I have to do.

Him: Hmm. (Silence)

You: What does that mean?

You'll notice that here the boyfriend's silence is being perceived in an aggressive manner as if it indicated annoyance or anger. This is what it would have meant if the girlfriend was silent. So, while silence can be a powerful tool for audiences, it can also be an effective, albeit slightly conflicting tool for other instances as well, which is why it is important to clarify silences, when appropriate.

10. Volume

How loudly you choose to speak is also a big deal, and can also help with the attention of the audience—louder vocal projections can be authoritative and grab your attention, but using a really low voice can result in higher levels of concentration.

11. Movement

Actual movement on stage can also help energize a crowd and boost your delivery. Remember, when you are delivering news you are effectively a performer.

Everything counts, starting from your voice to your choice of words, and even the way you are moving.

Cornerstones to Effective Communication

Now while the above-listed issues deal with the external aspects of how your speech will be perceived as you deliver it, there are also internal aspects that one should keep in mind. These aspects help form the integrity of a speech and ensure that on delivery, communication is not just considered palatable but rather is welcomed by the masses.

Honesty

Honesty is about being true in what you say, to be clear and straightforward without sugar coating an issue. This is important because if you are busy trying to save someone from the truth, you are going to have a hard time communicating to them what is actually going on.

Take for instance a boss-employee relationship. Your employee has been doing very poorly, and you have been told multiple times from a higher level that they need to better or they will be fired. Because you have a hard time communicating effectively and because complete honesty is something you struggle with every time you sought to explain or instruct him. Now, because his work has suffered continuously, your employee is being let go.

Do you see how your lack of honestly acted against the whole issue and how even with the best intentions true absolute communication is impossible in the absence of honesty? Remember, you can practice empathy and compassion when you speak; that is a laudable quality and one we'll tackle in the next chapter. But you need to be honest and clear for the sake of the person you are speaking to and yourself.

Authenticity

Authenticity is another important factor in effective communication. It may look similar to honesty but is quite different. Not only does authenticity require honesty, it also requires a sense of being true to oneself. This is extremely important for romantic relationships and friendships where failure to stand on one's own truth will lead to one being bound to a continuous *Groundhog D*ay scenario, where you'll find yourself continually having to pretend that you are okay with something that you are not really okay with.

Think of it like this. You really like this guy, and he happens to be a massive opera fan. To get to know each other better, you lie and tell him you love the opera too. You have been dating for over five years now, as you have found that you have a lot of things in common. However, you were never able to grow to like the opera as the high register and pitch triggers a migraine attack. He doesn't know this, and every time he wants to do something special he gets you opera tickets, which in turn you have to either try to avoid or suffer through. This leads to him thinking you don't appreciate his thoughtfulness.

Do you see how powerful authenticity can be? If you aren't true to yourself, and you allow that to form any kind of communicative basis you are moving forward with a fractured base, which at literally any point of your life could fracture and lead to mistrust and resentment. Which would really not be a good thing!

Integrity

Integrity is the opposite of being hypocritical. When you become someone, whose word has weight and values, you are also showing the world and more importantly, the people you are communicating with, that you are worthy of their trust. In today's political climate, it is not surprising that organizations and employees, specifically, are having a hard time trusting management and their leaders. The environment that we are currently existing in is spoiled with all the wrong kinds of leadership. Currently, communication lacks transparency and authenticity. This is because the objective of this communication is no longer to actually communicate truths but rather to use, and if necessary abuse workers, voters, friends, and family all with the intent of bettering one's own standing.

Since it can be a pretty tricky road, why don't we help you out a bit and give you a few quick tips that will help you ensure that you are acting with integrity?

1. Tell Your Own Story

So, when you are out there trying to be honest and true to yourself, it's easy to sometimes slip up and want to take the easy way out. One thing that will help keep you in line is if you are open with your own story. Talk to people about yourself and your vision, be it for a company or your own life—why? Because your vision is never going to include doing bad things and getting away with it. In fact, it will help reinforce your integrity to build on who you aspire to be.

2. Be Open to Change

Now, this is also important because stagnating in what you thought was right is an easy way to fall behind. Truths may not change, but rights and values do. You have to keep this in mind if you are to grow and develop as an individual.

3. Talk About the Good Stuff

Next, is reinforcement. Remember how we talked about Pavlov's dog earlier in the book, and how strong a role reinforcement played. The same applies to you. If you keep openly talking about the good things you've done, you can actually scare yourself away from the bad!

4. Be Real

And then there is being real. In any situation, your authenticity and honesty play a big role in establishing trust and conviction, both of which are important for someone who is seeking to be the best version of themselves. That is what you are doing because integrity goes beyond calm, cool logic. It deals with the big stuff like ethics and fairness, and they have to be a part of who you are.

Love

And finally, we are back to dealing with love or compassion. We spoke a little bit about how important love and empathy can be when it comes to constant communication. When we love someone, we try to ensure that they receive what is best for them. Love is a powerful tool. Not only does it help us understand the situations around us better, it also allows us to be better ourselves. If you love or care for someone, you will find that you are less likely to be judgmental or gossipy about them which are two of the biggest not to do's in terms of communication.

Think of it like this. If you see your best friend throwing a screaming fit, would you walk away saying, "what a drama queen," or would you be more likely to tell other people to back off as you try to find out what is going on, and why she is acting like that?

Our vote is on the latter. You see love gives us the ability to empathize instantly and that is super important when you are trying to explain something to someone or when you are trying to deliver any piece of information. There was an American surgeon a few years ago who went viral for talking out about DUI crash victims. He explained how before he delivered the bad news to the parents he would take the time to go through the victim's Facebook or other social media pages so he could see them with more love and compassion when he explained what had happened to the parents. This helped them in processing their grief.

This compassion is an element of love, which allows people to invest in their delivery, which is something we all should be doing!

Delivery Kryptonite: What NOT to Do

If you are speaking and people aren't listening to you, then there is something very wrong with the way you are speaking. Why do we say that? Well for starters, the human voice is a power tool, which in conjunction with non-verbal cues can be wielded to mean any number of things.

The human voice can start wars. The human voice can end them. We can crush a person's dreams or build them. Is there really anything more powerful than the human voice when wielded properly?

This automatically tells us one thing—if you are struggling to hold your audience's attention as you deliver information, as you communicate with them, you are doing something wrong. But what?

There are probably a million and one things you have been doing, and it's hard to identify what is the one thing that is alienating the audience. But it's not hard to go through a list to explore the common factors which are known to cause breaks in communication and then figure out what we've been doing wrong— right?

So, let's do that.

Do you feel you're up for it?

Or have you just taken in too much information, as it is? It is okay if you aren't. Take a nap or play a round of Candy Crush—we'll still be here when you to come back. But when you are ready, make sure you are coming back with a fresh mind, ready to take in and analyze the information being given.

Ready to go now?

Awesome!

Here we go!

1. Gossip

When you are dealing with someone who gossips, how much stock do you put in what they say? Think about it. Do you trust their words at face value? Do their words and actions leave you suspicious, and you're not quite sure how much of their opinion or statement you should believe, and you don't know how much is just made up? And what's worse you also don't know how much you can trust them because a person who gossips about others, would also gossip about you the second they had a chance.

Gossip ruins the inherent fabric of trust because even if someone is talking about something true in a "gossipy" manner, you automatically want to limit your own communications with that person because you are scared that you'll be their next target. Instead, if you have a concern of some sort and want to represent it, do so without presenting judgment to the person concerned. Judgment is the core issue here, and psychological studies show that over 60 percent of conversations between adults are about gossip, and if over 60 percent of the time you are being seen to pass judgment, how does that reflect on you?

Judgment

The next major "no, no" is being judgmental. The problem here though is that we are all judgmental. Yes, even you. Think about it. Every day when you step outside the house for a jog, or a grocery run, or to go to work, you might see around yourself hundreds, if not thousands of people, and as you look at them even for the briefest moment, you judge them.

Now judgment can be triggered by any number of things, starting from one's race, one's outfit, what kind of hairstyle they have, or what kind of glasses they are wearing. In one split millisecond, we capture a bunch of information and then put it into predetermined slots. If one is not well dressed they are either a druggie or homeless if one is well dressed, they are a hotshot, or if one is Asian, they are good at math. These constant broad generalizations may seem harmless when you start doing them in your head, but they are crippling.

A great method that many psychologists recommend is the DUAL method.

First off, Don't judge. If you see yourself judging, stop yourself and reprimand yourself, immediately. And while it's not always easy to be able to identify all the times that we have been judgmental, it is important that we try to observe and prevent it from happening. When you catch yourself judging someone, replace the judgment with *U*nderstanding. Try to empathize with them and understand where they are coming from. If someone is homeless, don't immediately label them good for nothing. Try to imagine what kind of hardships they must be facing and if possible strike up a conversation. Conversations help us overcome a lot of the pre-held biases that we are raised with, particularly when it comes to racial discourse. Once you have tried your best to understand them and what they are doing, move on to *A*cceptance. By accepting a person for who they are as opposed to trying to constantly change them to fit in with your definition of acceptable or normal, you are opening yourself up to the concept of diversity. Once you do that, you'll find it much easier not to be judgmental to begin with. To finish off though, you need *L*ove. This isn't the romantic kind of love that we are on about. Here, love means unconditional empathy, where you feel for a person, and you care about them regardless of their differences. Do you think you can try it?

Remember, it's okay to take it slowly. The fact that you are trying is the most important thing of all.

Negativity

Negativity is like viral misery. Not only does it breed more negativity, but it also hinders the progress of any

80

positive emotion that is within its ambit. So why are we always so negative? Why can't we be uber positive like Phoebe Buffay? Well, because our biology won't allow it. You see our brains are hardwired to think of things in terms of negativity. This is because we perceive negativity as a threat and try to work harder to defend against it.

Bummer, isn't it?

Honestly, more than you realize, negativity translates very poorly in verbal communication. So, if you are trying to get someone to do something, telling them about all the bad things that will happen if they don't do it is a lot less effective than telling them about all the good things that would happen if they did.

So how do we move away from negativity and make more room for positivity?

Well, one way is to work on the vocabulary that we use.

Let's start with a quick example. You are in charge of monitoring new employees, and one of them constantly messes up their work. Instead of focusing on the mistakes they are making and berating them by saying, "This is the worst report I've seen all my life, what on earth were you thinking! Did you even go to school?"

Try saying that positively, like, "Hey Brad, I want to discuss something with you. Do you have a minute? I was going through the report you sent me, and I'm afraid it doesn't quite meet company standards. I'll have Karen send you a sample draft and would really appreciate it if you could redo the report and submitted it to me by Friday."

The reason this is such a better option is because not only are you commiserating with Brad, you are also helping him figure out why his work isn't meeting standards by showing him a sample draft. You are also providing him with a deadline which is important because it shows him that even though you are phrasing it as a question, you mean business, and you are still in charge.

Overcoming negativity isn't as hard as people make it out to be. All you have to do is be willing to acknowledge that it's a problem and you need to start doing something about it. You can do that, right?

Complaining

Another common problem you'll come across once you start addressing negativity in communication is the tendency to complain. If when you are speaking, you are constantly bringing forth problems that you have identified and while that in itself isn't problematic, how you are phrasing them is.

Remember how we said that your brain is wired to go for the negative. Well, one of the reasons is because you complain—a lot. When your mind is trying to find a solution, and you provide it by complaining, what you are doing is teaching your brain that the way to solve a problem is to complain. The next time your brain senses a problem it goes into autopilot and—yes, you got it, complains.

And you know what's worse? Research from Stanford University[1] has shown that complaining causes your brain, or more specifically your hippocampus, to shrink. Which is really bad because the hippocampus is the part of your brain that does all the problem solving!

Excuses

The next major issue that tampers with your ability to actually deliver when it comes to any form of communication is excuses. Now there is a marked difference between explanations and excuses. An excuse

---

[1] http://www.talentsmart.com/articles/How-Complaining-Rewires-Your-Brain-for-Negativity-2147446676-p-1.html

is like an explanation that went wrong. On the one hand, you have a problem without a solution, and on the other, you don't even have an explanation or understanding of why it happened.

When it comes to being a leader or a boss, excuses can be extremely damaging both to a country's credibility and also to the morale of the other people around you. So how do you avoid making excuses? For starters, that isn't the only question you need to be asking—you need to ask how you are going to stop making excuses and how you can stop your employees and others making excuses.

As for yourself, you need to stop every time you make an excuse and attempt to evaluate what is causing you to react in this manner. What are the facts, what are you afraid of, and why are you afraid of it?

Once you manage to go through all that you'll find that there are often very valid reasons why something has happened. If there wasn't a valid reason, then the odds are that you are dealing with some sort of shortcoming in yourself. Were you procrastinating? Were you inefficient? What was the problem? Narrow down the issue and then move forward. Once you have identified the issue, you now need to find a way to solve it. If you were procrastinating you need to find a way to avoid it.

Try using a set routine, or have someone hold you accountable. The main point is to be proactively involved in the correction of the issue.

Once you have managed to do that you're good to go! But hold on, you haven't fixed the issue for your audience yet. How do you prevent them from making excuses? A technique that generally works well with children and employees is to give them room to make mistakes and help them understand that there's nothing wrong with mistakes. They will then tend to become more forthcoming and elect to actively express problems rather than hide them or make excuses.

First, you need to fix your own tendency to make excuses and then follow that up by showing the people you are speaking to that the same applies to them.

Dogmatism

You know how they say, that talking to some people can be the same as talking to a brick wall? Yeah, those people—everyone knows one of them, and frankly, if you don't, the odds are you are that person. (Sorry!)

Now, the official definition of dogmatism is simple—it's a tendency to lay down rules of notions which are perceived and promoted as undeniable fact with little to no regard for the consideration or opinions held by others.

Simply put, it's the idea that you are always right, to the point where you can't listen to anyone else at all.

Dogmatism is obviously a problem. But I don't think any of us really realize how big of a problem it is until the whole family is home for dinner, and you have that one uncle who is shoving his dogmatic opinions down everyone's throats. Yup, you got it—politics and religion and all those theological debates that everyone has personal views on suddenly become the central focus.

Now for years, you've been trying to deal with these issues by a combination of distraction and superfast ninja skills to help preserve your mental sanity, but now that you are older and wiser, you probably want to have a more concrete solution. You can't keep playing hot potato with your sister to distract people anymore.

So, what is the solution?

Well, there are multiple different things you can do to help with this issue, but let's first try to erase the dogmatism you have. After all, you are the communicator here, and your actions will be reflected in the audience.

Firstly, try to focus on commonalities. No matter how

different a person's thought process is unless you are dealing with Ed Gein and his skinsuit proclivity, the odds are you'll be able to find some common ground. This is what you need to focus on.

Now, let's say you belong to a core Catholic family, and you bring your Muslim girlfriend over for dinner. Your Dad begins preaching about the core tenets of Christianity and how it is the one true religion. How do you deal with this?

Why not try something basic, like saying, "Actually Dad, did you know that Islam is also an Abrahamic religion, and they also consider Christ to be a prophet?"

In bringing forth a commonality between the two supposedly opposing groups, you are forcing your Dad to realize that there is common ground. Your job is to then build on that and to keep talking about how the two religions also have other things in common.

It's cool how you knew to do that, right? But how do you ensure you always know how to? Well, you won't always know, but you can increase the probability a lot by expanding the circle of people you mix with and exposing yourself to different perspectives. But the most important thing is to do all of that with respect. Remember, dogmatic people are almost always super moody and arrogant. If you focus on winning and rubbing it in their face instead of being respectful of their thoughts as you guide them to another, you will do more damage than good. So always remember to be gentle and kind even with your words. After all, your words have an impact.

Exaggeration

Do you know what else you really need to avoid?

Embellishments. I mean, we totally understand that it can be pretty tempting to add a little spice to a story to maybe make it a little scarier or a little funnier. But this tendency to exaggerate could become rooted in your mind and cause you to exaggerate every little problem to the point where you act like the world is ending.

I know what you're thinking. It's not like you mean anything by it. You're just joking or making a point— right? Well, be that as it may, every time you do so you create unnecessary stress on your own mind and soul, and that in turn starts to take root in your consciousness. This means that at some point you start believing it!

How do you avoid crossing that line?

To start with, try to avoid the following three things:

1. Overgeneralizing

2. "Doom-enizing"

3. Jumping to Conclusions

With the first, the logic is simple; the more you generalize, the more you concentrate negativity. If something bad happens to you and then you follow up by telling yourself that bad things "always" happen to you, and then you start believing it. This sort of distorted thinking is key to negative thoughts, and we're trying to avoid those, remember?

Now, on to number two, "Doom-enizing" is when you portray every little problem as if it's the end of the world, like telling yourself you'll never be happy again after a bad breakup. Look, bad stuff happens, and no one is saying it's not bad, but you need to be able to identify what is doom inducing and what is two bottles of whiskey and a bad cry.

And finally, you have the whole issue of jumping to conclusions. Generally, this is a byproduct of overgeneralizing and dogmatic thinking. Because you are so sure that you are right, and you have already exaggerated your facts to fit your narrative, you are now also coming to conclusions that fit in with that narrative and your impending sense of catastrophe. It's like a vicious circle. All these bad habits are feeding each other, and you are letting it happen!

Lying

Finally, you are dealing with lies, and trust me when I say this is the worst thing you can do during any form of communication. Now, we're not talking about while lies, like "Babe, of course you haven't put on weight!" We're talking about the ugly stuff, which may seem insignificant in the moment but is extremely damaging in the long run—such as "No, I wasn't hurt by what you said." "Yes, I am happy to leave, and I don't mind giving up my job to follow you."—you know the heavy stuff.

Lying is particularly dangerous because if you happen to be dealing with someone who happens to lie as well, you won't be able to figure out when you are dealing with the truth and when you are not—which is problematic. It's a lot worse though when you are the one who is doing the lying. If your company gets caught in lies, you are effectively setting yourself up for failure. Think of Komen for the Cure which was a company which claimed its mission was to save lives and end breast cancer forever. The company later sustained a loss of almost a hundred million dollars when it came out that they were affiliated with cancer-inducing products. And you have to remember that trust once lost is almost impossible to rebuild!

Play it smart—don't lie!

Are You on the Right Track?

So, now that you are all but done and have an in-depth understanding of what Good Delivery deals with do you want to run through a few quick questions to make sure you're on track?

Great!

First off, are you identifying your target audience? Remember, knowing who your target audience *is,* is the key to ensuring you are using the correct method of delivery.

Second, are you being polite? Remember, courtesy is a basic need for effective communication, which means if you aren't nice, the odds are you won't get what you want!

Third, are you doing the whole overgeneralization thing again? Yes? That needs to stop immediately. You're not going to get anywhere if your story is all fluff and no substance.

Fourth, are you being objective? People find it hard to be objective or neutral about topics they care deeply about, and this is why it is super important that you as the communicator are consciously avoiding bias.

Remember, a good communicator conveys ideas not opinions.

And fifth, are you or your audience being silent? What does it mean? Now, silence is a funny thing. It can mean that you are so invested that you are listening intently. On the other hand, it can be a form of aggressive emotional abuse, which is really bad—how do you figure out the difference?

Initially, check to see if there is a pattern. Is it because they have run out of words, or is it because *you* may be quite relentless when you are communicating and causing people to shut down when they try to talk to you? If it's not you, then you need to find a way to let your significant other know that what they are doing is brutal and not okay.

Initially, you will want to be abrasive, but the best way to deal with it is to have a calm, reasonable conversation, show them that you are not fighting them and are willing to be spoken to and wish to solve this problem.

To-Do Drills—Your OFFICIAL Action Items

We're officially done with all the how's and what's—meaning we are ready to move on to the more proactive bit of the program. Delivery is an active process, and the only way you can ensure you will be able to improve your delivery is if you start to include these issues into your daily routine, and proactively practice them until you have them down pat.

Ready?

Since delivery is such a broad topic we'll do a little more than five action items—don't panic though, you don't' have to do them all at once! You can slowly build them into your routine, but remember that these are mere guidelines. The theoretical application and the actual application are going to differ, so feel free to adapt things as you see fit!

Here we go!

1. Keep to the Core Message

It's easy to accidentally move away from the central topic, particularly when you are dealing with a broad, general topic. Most topics involve a general theme more than an actual event or point, and it is up to the communicator to ensure that their message contains the kind of information the audience needs to receive. So be clear and stick to one core message!

2. Build in NO MORE than three Supporting Points

However, no discussion is sustained by one point alone. The best thing that you can do is to shortlist three points which you believe support your argument or topic and use them to build the message you want to present.

Just remember, don't go for an overload of information—three points are more than enough!

3. Be Kind and Tactful as You Speak

Another obvious little action item is to work on your kindness. We've talked about the importance of kindness before and will do so again in the following chapter. Remember that it plays a key role in how your message is received, and as such cannot be skipped over.

4. Keep Your Blood Flowing

One other thing that many good communicators do is to walk or stay as they present what they are saying. The constant movement helps the blood to keep flowing and the audience from feeling bored as they tend to follow much of your activity mentally.

5. Use Props

On a side note, always try to keep props handy. Having a prop allows you to engage with something while you are speaking and that helps embed certain moments of your speech in your audience's mind.

6. Always Maintain Eye Contact

Eye contact is another important factor that you can't do without. It tells your audience that you are speaking specifically to them and that in turn helps you form a connection with your audience.

7. Be Brief but Complete

And finally, your last action item for this chapter is to ensure that you have completed your speech or your intended communication in the briefest and yet fullest way possible. Remember, our attention only lasts for so long, and a communicator will finish speaking before we can take a mental hike.

Got it?

Awesome!

Go practice now!

Chapter Three: Engage with Empathy

"When you show deep empathy towards others their defensive energy goes down and positive energy replaces it. That's when you can get more creative in solving problems."—Stephen Covey

Have you ever tried to understand the word, empathy?

Like really try to understand it.

No, don't just try to use it in a sentence. Yes, we know it's an adjective.

But what does it mean?

What does empathy look like? How tangible is it? What are the factors that define it?

That's a lot of questions, isn't it?

Let's tone this entire interrogation down a notch, and come back to the first question we asked—what does "empathy" mean.

In a word? Empathy means to "experience." You know

the old saying, "walk a mile in someone else's shoes?" It means, to be them for the day so you can see, hear, feel, and think like they do. Empathy is the same.

Empathy means to feel as if you *are* them—to be mad when they are mad, to feel sad when they are sad, not to feel sorry for them (that's sympathy).

It's simple really—imagine being really, really self-absorbed and selfish—that's not empathy.

Now, imagine the opposite. Imagine being kind, and compassionate, and looking at what someone is going through and thinking of it from their perspective. This *is* empathy.

The reason that empathy is so important though is because empathy allows you to communicate with flexibility or adaptability. Since empathy allows you to step into another person's shoes, empathetic communicators, in turn, can use this newfound knowledge to shape how they deal with the person in front of them.

It's like when you make a "Yo Mama" joke, only to later find out that the person you told that joke to, lost their mother last year—automatically your brain realizes that joke, in this particular context was wildly inappropriate.

This realization, although it is admittedly a little late in this case, is empathetic. As you'll see by the end of this chapter, empathy is a key part of any communication, not just because it helps create less friction, but more importantly because it enables you to understand that the value of all communication is based on its context instead of the communication itself. Pouring yourself a drink, only makes sense if you are pouring it into a container of some sort. Pouring 50-year-old scotch on the sidewalk as you walk home is just a waste. So even if you are using the same words or the same actions, your communication means different things when applied to different areas or people.

The importance and value of empathy are obviously not up for debate, but there are a few other questions we need to understand. How does one develop empathy? Is it natural? How does it tie into shared identity and how do we apply it? What is it made up of? When does it kick in? When is empathy of particular importance?

And suddenly we're back to the 101 questions. Let's take these one at a time.

Ready?

Grab your popcorn. Here we go!

Natural Forms of Empathy

First off, let's try to figure out how empathy fits into our day-to-day lives.

Now, don't be fooled. Empathy isn't all one big bubble of stuff. It's actually made up of two major empathetic factors, which together combine to form what we broadly refer to as empathy.

Before we get into any of that though, we need to be able to distinguish between empathy and sympathy. Think about it like this. "you are shopping at Target and come across a tag that says, "Made in China." This reminds you of a news article that you saw a few weeks ago where they talked about the awful work conditions in Chinese sweatshops. Suddenly, you are overcome with sorrow; you feel bad for the people in the sweatshops. This NOT empathy. You are feeling sorry for them; you feel bad on their behalf. This is sympathy.

Empathy is when you are thinking of what it would feel like to be them, a worker in a sweatshop who gets paid less than three dollars a day for over twelve hours of labor. This particular form of empathy is called *emotional empathy*—you are feeling how the other person feels.

Emotional empathy can develop from one of two ways. One way is to be able to feel what they feel, with the key element being attention. The more you pay attention, the better you will be able to connect with the other person, and, that is when you build "rapport." This form of connective empathy is commonly referred to as social empathy and is super important in all relationships, but particularly when you are working towards a common goal. Social empathy works best when accompanied by empathetic concern which is the more proactive part of empathy. Your rapport and connectivity with the person are triggering a need to do something about it. This could be something as simple as making them a cup of tea and listening to them or taking someone to a hospital. That's really all it takes because at its core the basis of empathetic concern is the connectivity of feelings and actions.

The second type of empathy is ***cognitive empathy*** which tends to center mostly around awareness. You don't have to feel the way another person feels to have cognitive empathy. All you really need to do is be able to think like them. It's like knowing what another person will like. Say you like vanilla ice-cream and your partner likes strawberry. You don't have to like strawberry ice-cream to know that when he's getting a milkshake he'd probably prefer a strawberry flavored one.

Combining the two types of sympathy allows for amazingly fluid communication.

Why?

Because now, not only are you thinking like the person you are speaking to, and therefore, understanding where they are coming from, you are also feeling how they feel, and acting based on that. The stronger your empathetic skills are, the stronger your relationships will be!

Absolutely mind-blowing, isn't it?

Shared Identity and Communication

The reason that empathy is preached high and low whenever it comes to communication is because empathy can change the course of almost everything. A well-phrased statement or a kind nod can be the difference between keeping a job or walking away in search of kindness, and sometimes it can even be the difference between life and death.

Empathy plays an active role here because it is empathy that either creates a sense of shared identity where you treat the individual you are communicating with as one of your own or where you identify them as "similar" or "alike" and form a sort of mental kinship. The absence of empathy on the other hand alternatively creates a sense of "otherness" when you don't consider the individual to be part of your *in-group* and as such don't trust them as much.

It's basically a sense of "us" versus "them."

Before we move on to anything else, I want you to try to identify five major instances you have noticed this kind of grouping in modern day life.

Let's start with *your* own life. Rewind a bit and take

yourself back to high school. Who were you? You were either a cool kid, or you weren't. Here the distinction was clear. The cool kids, the jocks, the cheerleaders etc., all seemed to form one *in-group*. Anyone who didn't fit that bill was automatically sorted to the outgroup.

The sad thing is—we never really grow out of high school so *in-group, out-group* concepts tend to take over everywhere. If you're working in customer service, it's floor staff versus management. In politics, it's Democrats versus Republicans. If it's at university, it's departments versus each other. The list of mini internal battles is infinite, as is the impact this concept of shared identity has on communication.

Let's look at each side individually.

Communication in IN-Groups and OUT-Groups

In-group communication is easy. Because individuals tend to feel a connection or a bond with another set of people, they are inclined to find them more trustworthy, and communication that takes place between in-group members is better received and considered to be worth more attention.

In contrast, out-group conversation is like bad tasting

medicine because we don't want it. We move away from it so that the information fails to register to the fullest extent and even where it does the will to ensure that it is followed perfectly falls short. The sense of detachment is what causes the communication to fail, and it also causes a perceived dip in communication quality. Not only do you not want to follow instructions, your brain is also justifying this by telling you that the instructions are more difficult.

The positivity with which in-group communication is perceived is therefore critical to its impact. This is why lower middle-class white Americans are more likely to want a white presidential candidate who speaks in simple sentences, as opposed to a well-educated person of color, whose political policies are actually *more* beneficial to that class of people.

So, long story short, we need empathy. Without it, we are delivering substandard communication which may not seem critical if you are a marketing team dealing with product placement, but is super important when you are a doctor taking a patient's medical history.

Cultivating Empathy

We know empathy is great and all, but let's get to the crux of the matter. How do we create empathy?

To start, you need to slow down a bit and go back to what we were talking about a little earlier. Remember how we said there were two types of empathy? And one dealt with thought, while the other dealt with feelings and actions?

Well, let's start with thought this time. To cultivate empathy, you need to be able to first identify and apply perspective. This is called **attribution**. The ability to do so allows individuals to quickly pick up information which is relevant to the situation or audience and calculate how best to deliver their message, so it resonates with the audience.

This brings us to **accommodation** which is the one thing we overlooked here—the tangible expression of the element of care. Think of it like this. To know what another party needs or wants to hear is one thing, but changing your own approach to make room for those needs, to cater to those wants, that's different. That is accommodation.

Pro Tip: If you are trying to consciously enhance your empathy levels and aren't sure how, know this—the two things that significantly boost empathy—exposure and an excellent vocabulary.

How?

A good vocabulary gives you more range in how you can build your conversations. The more languages you know, the better your comprehension of other cultures and the more words you know of your own language, the better your ability to get your thoughts across will be.

Exposure, on the other hand, is important for obvious reasons. The more you mix with people, and the more you travel, the more you can practice your skills. Contrary to popular thinking, empathy is not the same in all languages and cultures. What may be considered empathetic in one would be sympathetic to others. You need to give yourself the opportunity to see and learn what empathy means in different cultures and act accordingly!

Building Empathetic Communication in Day-to-Day Life

Just understanding that empathy is important or figuring out the basic structure of how to create artificial empathy isn't enough. We communicate with so many different people from so many different walks-of-life every single day, that more often than not we forget that there are certain goals that our communication has to meet.

We need to make sure that when communicating, we have done so in a manner that is understood. Simply speaking and walking away without noting whether or not the recipient of the information has been able to absorb or process what we said, isn't effective. Neither is communication which is stunted due to either poor execution of instructions or because of the personal limitations of the subject to whom instructions are delivered.

If we cannot see how our communication is perceived by the individuals we are attempting to communicate with, and how they are reacting, or are likely to react to it on an individual basis, we are failing to have empathetic communication.

An easy way to avoid this is to work on five lessons on empathy, that will help keep your journey with empathy on track.

Lesson One: Context-based Adaptation

The first lesson you need to learn is that empathy is subjective. As we've said before, the nature and the construct of what is considered empathy tends to change based on the circumstances you are in, and as such, must continuously be adapted to fit in with its surroundings.

This kind of adaptation can refer to a variety of things. It can refer to words you are choosing to use or even how you use them.

Let's clarify this with an example.

Let's say, you are the parent of two children, Jake aged 5, and a girl named Jessie, who is 4. Now, Jake and Jessie have drastically different personalities. Jake is obedient and loving but easily spooked. Jessie is selfish, greedy, and tends to act out when she doesn't get her way.

You need to take both of the kids to the doctor to get their flu shots, but you're not sure how to since Jake is likely to start crying in fear and Jessie is likely to start throwing a fit that will make it even more difficult to deal with both of them. As a parent, how do you use empathy to effectively communicate with the children in such a manner that you can get them to go and get the shot?

The first thing you need to do is to understand the context—who are you speaking to? Children, right? Are they capable of understanding medical mumbo jumbo? Unless Jake is secretly Sheldon Cooper, probably not, which means medical talk isn't going to be an effective way to deal with this situation.

Okay, now let's focus on each kid individually. Jake is loving and is prone to get upset when his sister is hurt or when you the parent seem to be in pain. As his weakness is fear, an empathetic way of dealing with this would be to give him a way to overcome it. Explain to Jake that because he is a big, brave boy he needs to come to the doctor with you and Jess, so the doctor can give him something that will help keep him, Jess and you safe from harm. The idea of being able to protect the people he cares about from harm would ideally offset his natural fear, and as such would help you get him to the doctor with minimum fuss.

Unfortunately, this same technique is not likely to work on Jess as she and Jake have drastically different personalities. Instead, try to use a more bribery-based technique to deal with her. As Jessie is more materialistic, use that to compel her to behave appropriately. Identify something she wants, such as candy or a toy, and tell her that if she gets through the whole appointment without throwing a tantrum, you'll take her to get whatever it is that she wants, and voila! Problem solved!

Lesson Two: Behind the Scenes of Common Communication

While we agree and understand that it is important that we adapt our speech pattern or the words we are using, to fit in with the needs of the audience, what is less clear is how we are to assess and then decide what to say and what not to say.

Try using the following questions to help you out here:

- Why do they need to hear it?
- What words should be used to send the message?
- Where do they need to hear it?
- Who do they need to hear it from?
- When is the message too long?
- How do they need to hear it?

Before we get into each of these questions, let's quickly note that all of what we are about to deal with has to do with non-verbal communication. This is super important because while the words we are choosing to use are important, it is equally important to know what not to say or when not to say it. So, as you go through each of these questions try to make a mental note of all the non-verbal cues that are being elicited as a byproduct.

Now, coming back to the main six questions.

Why do they need to hear it?

Say for instance you are dealing with someone who has an issue with racial equality and works for the KKK. Engaging them in conversation may not sound like the sanest thing to do, but in fact, they need to be made aware of what they are doing and the impact such actions have on actual human beings.

What words should be used to send the message?

The words that you choose to use are a big part of communication and often when dealing with difficult clients, one wrong word can lead to disaster.

The first thing you need to do is evaluate what type of person are you dealing with. Are they passive or authoritative? An authoritative person will not take well to being spoken to in an authoritative tone, whereas a passive person usually responds better to authority than to suggestion.

It's the difference between using can or may, or using a positive no versus a negative no. You need to choose and craft your sentences in a manner that makes them more palatable to the intended audience.

Where do they need to hear it?

Another thing that you could probably do well with remembering is that it's not always the right place to have a particular conversation. As a manager dealing with a belligerent employee, it might not be a good idea to rebuke him on the shop floor with customers and other employees listening in unless you are trying to make a point.

Empathetic communication seeks to be effective, so you need to ask yourself if the best and kindest way of doing what needs to be done is out in the open, or behind closed doors where he is more likely to be forthcoming about what happened and why.

Who do they need to hear it from?

Another thing you need to think about is if you are the

right person to be delivering the message. If someone you love is hurt in a drunk driving accident, you're probably not going to want to hear that news from the drunk driver in question, right?

So, who is speaking is equally if not more important than the message, as the core of empathetic communication is connectivity and rapport building.

When is the message too long?

Just as there is a place and time for all things, there is also a timer on the time allocated to discuss these things. A message ceases to be effective if the communication goes on for too long. At the same time, short one-word answers aren't always enough either. Speak and communicate but try to find a balance.

How do they need to hear it?

Particularly in today's world and environment, the mode of delivery seems to be essential to the understanding of how seriously or how important certain communication will be. Canadian professor and visionary, Marshall McLuhan, once said that the medium is the message. How we choose to impart a specific piece of knowledge is telling, in terms of how we the communicator perceives that message and how that message will be perceived.

Lesson Three: The Devil is in the Details

Unless you happen to be dealing with someone who has a photographic memory, your audience is unlikely to retain all or even most of the information that you will impart during communication. How much attention have you been paying to this book? Enough to be able to remember all of the key points laid out in Chapter One? Unlikely.

There is nothing wrong with that—that's normal.

Now let me ask you this. Since you aren't going to remember most of the discussion anyway, is it really important to focus on the details?

The answer is an unequivocal yes.

Because you won't remember everything, it is crucial that all of the details are as perfect as possible because there is no telling which particular bit will stick with your audience. If you cushion your amazing message with a bunch of off-the-topic tales, the audience is more likely to remember that you kept talking about off-topic issues, not your amazing message. Odds are, they will gloss right over it. Your words are like a renaissance painting come to life—with each sentence you are adding definition. Be gentle and be meticulous. Your audience deserves it!

Lesson Four: Self-Empathy

Because empathy seems to be all about putting oneself in another person's shoes and may seem like a demand to put yourself last in line when it comes to priorities, it's easy to slip down the "people pleaser" slope.

But here's the thing. Self-empathy is just as important as empathy for other people. Focusing on external expressions of empathy can be super harmful for your own mental health. The need to continually please or help people can prevent you from engaging in effective communication when you're dealing with a confrontational issue.

Besides, fake empathy is of no use to anyone, and it isn't just hard, it's impossible to feel for someone else if you aren't kind and compassionate enough to feel for yourself. Remember, true empathy stems naturally from compassion. It's not a farce you put up and do away with later.

As the communicator, you are in a position of leadership, and as such, you should accurately express what you feel so those you are talking to will have a clear understanding of what is happening and what reactions they can expect in the future for similar behavior. The more transparent you are in your communication, the more you'll see a reflection of that clarity in your audience.

Lesson Five: Unity

And finally, remember that your empathy needs to be an extension of you.

Keep in mind that communication is a two-way street, so you're not lobbing a ball of information across a fence and running away. You are standing there absorbing everything you say, just as much as your audience is—probably more because you are more invested in it.

Theologian, Peter Rollins, once said that *love letters always get to their destination.*

His logic was simple. Love letters, more than being intended for a specific target audience, are meant to have a specific objective. Their objective is to deliver themselves and the thoughts in them to an individual.

In Rollin's opinion, you are that individual. You write because words are pouring out of you. Similarly, your empathy must come from within naturally, because you are the first consumer, if you are faking it, the first person you are betraying is yourself.

Empathetic Living—Are you doing it Right?

Just knowing how to apply empathy isn't enough to boost your communication standards. There is a marked difference between knowing that you should be doing something and actually doing it. This is why we will go through some of the common activities that you as a communicator deal with regularly, and then teach you how to apply empathy so that you are better equipped the next time the opportunity arises.

Are you ready to get started?

You may want to grab a pen and paper for this bit if you want to take notes.

Here we go!

1. Are you practicing Empathy as you speak?

When you are speaking, such as at a meeting or perhaps on a talk show, or even just at a dinner table with friends, one of the first things you need to know is "who" you are speaking too. Knowing your target audience makes it that much easier to understand what to say, and what is an effective mode of transmission etc.

Come to think about it, there really isn't any such thing as a generic response. Every response is case specific. Say you are comforting a friend whose father died. What would you say? "I'm sorry for your loss," is pretty generic. But what if I told you this friend was abused by her father as a child. Is that still what you would say? Probably not.

Understanding who you are speaking to is going to go a long way to determine what you can say, and what you can't as well. Understanding what is worthwhile and what isn't is particularly effective in business, although it is strongly applicable everywhere.

Scenario:

You have a speech on procrastination that you need to deliver on to your boss and a handful of other senior managers, most of whom are known to be tardy. What is the best way to approach this topic? Should you be authoritative or friendly? Will you scold them and all procrastinators, condemning them and calling them inefficient? Can you find a way to jokingly and compassionately talk about some of the reasons why "we" are late and then explain how we can overcome those problems by doing X, Y, or Z?

Understanding where you stand with your audience helps you find a better way to explain the things that need to be said. You aren't shying away from the topic; you are merely supplying the requisite information in the manner in which they are most likely to accept and acknowledge it.

Sound good?

2. Is your writing empathetic enough?

Most of the logic you've just applied to your speaking metaphor also applies directly to your writing. An empathetic writer should be doing all the things a speaker is doing; only they need to do a little bit more.

When you are speaking, your content is backed up by a bunch of non-verbal communication you don't even realize that you're doing. Your hand gestures, the way your intonation changes, your facial expressions—all of these things add value and make your speech worthier.

When you are writing, you need to find a way to do this without having a direct audience.

So, what do you do?

For starters, you figure out your target audience; who

are they, what are they likely to respond to, what is it that they want, and how can I give it to them?

A great example of empathetic writing by a company is Procter and Gamble's "Best Job" campaign. The company, which produces a multitude of household products was targeting mothers and their notion of being invisible in their role of caretakers and mothers being the equivalent of a full-time job. Not only was the advertisement catchy and uplifting for moms, but it was also written in a way that told mothers they were valued, which of course led to a peak in sales. After all, who does the shopping in your house?

Writing isn't always about advertisements, though. Writing can be a part of your job if you are a journalist or an author. It can be part of your course work if you go to school or university. If you are in a relationship it could be a love letter, and in every aspect it is critical that you use your words to help identify and uplift, so as to give roots to the empathy you are trying to grow in your communication.

3. Are you listening with empathy?

We've already talked at length about how important empathetic listening is in chapter one, but we'll give you a quick recap anyway. Contrary to popular opinion, listening is as active an exercise as speaking. The attention to detail that is required when one is listening is actually higher than when you are a speaker. As a speaker, you are giving out information, whereas when you are listening you are both giving out multiple verbal and non-verbal cues, and at the same time taking in and processing information.

Active listening is a particularly important part of effective communication, and a part of active listening deals with having empathy for the speaker.

Imagine you are listening to your Uncle Tod, who is a hardcore Trump supporter talk about his political choices. You are a Democratic Socialist and prefer Bernie Sanders and hate the racist propaganda that your uncle's elected president is promoting. Will you be able to get anything from what your uncle is saying if all you can think of while he speaks is how badly you want to interrupt him and tell him what a horrible person his candidate is?

No! Of course not. But, if you want to, and if you choose, you can engage in empathetic listening where even if you don't agree with what your uncle is claiming, you can at least figure out where he is coming from, why he thinks the way he does and what lead him to vote for his candidate. In the long run, this would have more effect than the rant you were planning in your head.

4. Are you the you on Social Media that you would be in real life?

Another super important mode of communication in today's world is social media. Facebook, Instagram, Twitter, and even Snapchat to a considerable extent have replaced actual social interaction on the whole, and it's even more important now than ever before to practice empathy on social media.

When you get into an argument on social media, it's really easy to get nasty super-fast. Usually, this is because the individual on the other end when you are on social media doesn't really feel like a human being at all. They're more like an object or a thing—like a bot. You don't' necessarily attach feelings or emotions to them, but that doesn't mean what you're doing is right.

Social Media is a mode of communication just like the telephone, so be as kind on it as you would be to someone who calls to have a conversation. Remember your empathy should overshadow your anger or rage. That is the only way in which you'll be able to have mature conversations.

If you are having a fight with your partner and at some point, you realize you are both just screaming at each other. The reason you can't get through to each other is because you are both lacking empathy. Take a step back, hold on to your thoughts, put them in your back pocket and try to understand them for a minute. What are they saying? Why are they saying it? You won't win in a relationship by winning an argument. You win by preventing them with conversation.

5. Are you Judging?

And the last little thing you may have forgotten. When it comes to empathy, there is no room for judgment. Now, we know you wouldn't ever consciously set out to judge someone, but when you are dealing with someone if you don't try to empathize you will hold them against your standards, and that is judging.

To-Do Drills—Your OFFICIAL Action Items

Now that we're all caught up on how and what we need to be doing to be empathetic and effective communicators why don't we run you through a list of things to keep you in practice for the next two weeks, and hopefully forever after.

Remember, that practice makes perfect, and while empathy is naturally occurring, you will need to allow the whole process a little time before it can become second nature to you.

For now—let's run you through your drills!

1. Be empathetic at work!

You spend most of your waking hours surrounded by these people and end up spending over 80 percent of your year working with them and having conversations with them. That's a lot of time to spend with people you hate or dislike and what's more, it's really bad for your own mental health to be trapped in that mental prison.

Stop.

Take a deep breath and resolve to be kinder and nicer, to build a kinder narrative for them, and make excuses for them for just two short weeks. At the end of it you might not even have to fake it anymore!

2. Use empathy in social interactions!

Equally important are your interactions with the people around you in your day-to-day life. The smallest things like a smile on your way out the door, or a joke from your cabbie are things that can brighten your day because proximity has a serious impact on our lives.

So, use that knowledge. Do the same. Be kind and empathetic to the people you meet. You'll find that resolving to be kinder automatically makes your stress levels take a dive. Suddenly, you don't have to be mad because someone cut in line, you can make a mental excuse about how he's late for his first interview and couldn't help it. Remember kindness above all.

3. Real leaders have empathy!

And it doesn't end there! Empathy is a critical element

of good leadership. Multiple studies have shown[2] that empathy outshines almost every other leadership skill and is key to promoting commitment and cooperation in offices and workplaces. Twenty percent of employees are now being sent to empathy training and team building exercises to increase loyalty to the team and the company.

4. Be Kind to Yourself!

We spoke about self-empathy and its importance before, so we aren't going to go into depth on this matter, but do keep in mind that you have to put yourself first to be able to do this for anyone else.

5. Meditate!

And finally, this may seem a tad bit whimsical, but empathy and all that communication can take a toll on your psyche. It forces you to be continuously engaged,

---

[2] https://www.fastcompany.com/90272895/5-reasons-empathy-is-the-most-important-leadership-skill

and you don't want that. No one does really, but since you have to deal with it anyway, cleanse your mind and soul every so often just to make sure you aren't overwhelming yourself!

Okay?

What are you waiting for! Test it out!

Come on—off you go!

Chapter Four: Hone Your Honesty

"Open, honest communication is the best foundation for any relationship, but remember that at the end of the day, it's not what you say or what you do, but how you make people feel that matters the most."—Tony Hsieh

As we move forward, you'll soon come to realize that of all the things needed for effective communication the two most important are open and honest communications. And the logic behind this is fairly simple as well. Communication is a lot of constant, hard work. It's not like work where you get weekends off. You are communicating with people almost all the time, be it with friends and family, or with colleagues and strangers. You're always doing it.

This is why it's funny. After doing well over ten thousand hours of communicating, we still aren't anywhere near world-class standard. So, what are we doing wrong?

A lot of things, and we've already discussed them in the previous chapters, starting from proper listening to proper delivery of information and even underlying issues like empathy. The one thing we didn't cover in much detail is the value of honesty in terms of how to communicate correctly and effectively.

One of the biggest problems that we deal with particularly if we are in the minority end of the spectrum is how honest we should be when confronted. If you are a black man in today's America, this thought will come to mind quite often, particularly when dealing with the authorities, with police brutality being what it is. How honest should I be? Should I always push my point forward regardless of the situation? Or should I lie and let them feel better so they'll stop harassing me?

Quite a difficult choice, isn't it?

While there is no perfect answer to this particular scenario, you should of course always put your safety above any communication skill that you have learned. It's also important to softly start asserting yourself and your truth to begin bringing about an end to this kind of abuse of public authority. You need to use your voice and tell people what your truth is. They aren't going to know otherwise, and at the same time, you need to do so in a safe, stable manner where you are not fearful for your life.

But police brutality isn't the only time you've wondered about how honest you should be, and these nine steps will work amazingly well for situations like that. They are meant to equip you to help deal with situations in which you either don't know how to be honest or if you should be honest.

So, you're covered both ways.

Think of this as a reboot. What we are about to do is deal with all of your communication, honestly and openly as it should be dealt with, and restart the clock for those ten thousand hours. So, why don't we stop wasting time and show you how to perfectly hone those honesty skills.

Step One: Deep Listening

We've talked about listening before in depth, and I'm sure you think you know all there is to know about listening but hold on for a second. Do you see what you are doing right now? You are making a presumption. Your presume that you have learned all there is to learn about listening, and you don't need to know anything else—because you think there is nothing left to learn. Here is the problem with this—you *refused* to listen based on a presumption.

While you may be right, and you may theoretically know all there is to know, you have not been able to apply that learning well enough. This shows that your ability to listen is still superficial or shallow, whereas what you need to cultivate is deep listening. So, why is deep listening important? Because often what a person says on the surface and what they are trying to convey isn't the same.

Take the following situation for instance:

There are five people in a sales team called Insurgent, which is managed by Jake. They are Cassie, Penny, John, Mark, Lewis, and Jake himself. John and Jake are brothers and Jake is best friends with Mark and Cassie who is Jake's girlfriend. Penny has been dealing with Mark being inappropriate with her for over three months now. As there is no formal HR, she initially spoke to John since he was a fellow employee and then had two conversations with Jake where he tried to explain the issue. But John had already told Jake it wasn't a problem, and Jake is now refusing to act on it, telling Penny she is overly sensitive. The conversation is between you, Lewis and Cassie.

Penny: I hate talking to the boss; there is literally no point.

You: What do you mean?

Penny: He's impossible to deal with. He doesn't even care about the things that are going on in the office?

You: He doesn't care about the office?

Penny: Obviously not, or he'd actually take office problems seriously instead of just listening to his brother all the time.

You: His problem is that he only listens to his brother.

Now, *prima facie* you've done all the right things. Your conversation was reflective; you prompted for more information. You did it all—so where did you go wrong? Well, you were listening superficially, and you took things at face value instead of adding context. Ask yourself why Penny was feeling that way. Why does she believe the boss doesn't care? The ability to understand the root problem is central to the proper establishment of honest communication. Next time, listen with your heart as well as your ears.

Step Two: Ownership Attitude

The next most important thing is owning up to your own behavior, so you know how you were trying to figure out if you should be honest, or if you should lie in case the person you are speaking to can't "take it." What you just did right there is act like a blame-thrower. You took the fact that there are adverse reactions to your communication at times, and you decided it was because the person couldn't take your honesty. Automatically, you are absolved of guilt.

Or are you?

Think of this in the context of the following scenario:

You have been best friends with Mary for fifteen years now. Recently, Mary has been dating a guy named Ahmed who is five years younger than you. During a conversation, you decided to tell Mary that you think she's stupid to be dating Ahmed, as they are so different and because she's having such a hard time in the relationship. Mary takes offense to your statement. The argument goes as follows:

You: It's never going to work out, so I really don't see why you're wasting your time.

Mary: That's not fair. I really love him, and I want this to work out!

You: You've said that about every guy you've dated, and let's be real, that's like ten different guys a year. Just move on.

Mary: I can't move on!

You: You haven't even tried! You two don't even speak the same language!

Mary: You just hate him because he's Muslim!

You: I couldn't care less. It's not about Ahmed being Muslim; it's about him not being right for you, and you refusing to admit it!

Mary: Well, you're wrong. Go away!

Okay, now that was a pretty helpful conversation, wasn't it?

Note the sarcasm.

Look at the conversation. Whether you are right or wrong is beyond the point. Acting like a school-yard bully and labeling it brutal honesty is not a helpful mode of communication and is an entirely futile exercise. The only thing you have done in this process is alienate your own best friend, and what's worse is you are blaming her for the exchange. When people are discussing a problem, it is narcissistic to think that the solution or the problem you are seeing is something they haven't seen already, or that you are telling them something they don't know. When people are trying to tell you something, they are trying to be heard, and you have failed that. You were so busy explaining how you were right that you weren't able to hear or understand Mary's needs.

The first thing that you need to do in this instance is to learn how to admit that you are problematic. Your behavior is overbearing, and you will not be able to change it until you take ownership. Admit you are wrong, recognize the problem and the pattern, and then move on.

Step Three: Purpose

Now that you have acknowledged and realized that there are issues with your behavior and your approach to honesty let's try to figure out the central purpose of an honest and open conversation—achieving a specific goal or purpose. Now, as we've said before, honesty is a critical part of achieving a goal. Its a central part of being productive. But how are you going to be productive, if your communication is too harsh to begin with?

Look at the following scenarios and try to understand the primary differences:

You are a manager of an upscale boutique hotel where you often have celebrity guests check in under aliases. Recently the names of the celebrity guests have been leaked out to various tabloids, and this is causing the hotel to lose business. You have been assigned to speak to all floor staff and assess where this leak is coming from and put a stop to it.

Conversation One:

You: I can't believe that we have to do this but someone on the floor has been leaking private information about hotel guests to the media, and once we find out who it is you are fired! And if we find out that any of you knew and didn't do anything about it, you're fired too!

Okay, now how do you think your staff is going to react to this announcement? You have effectively told them that one of their friends and colleagues has been messing up and is going to lose their job because of it. Regardless of whether or not the slip-ups were intentional or not, or if they were facing a financial crisis, you proclaimed that anyone who knows of the incident, regardless of whether or not they come forward now, are also going to be fired! How forthcoming do you think your employees are going to be?

Your communication has utterly failed its purpose of identifying and stopping the leaks.

In contrast, consider this:

Conversation Two:

You: The hotel has been very disappointed to find that there is one of us who is not being as considerate of the privacy of our guests as we usually are. We are going to try to find an amicable way to solve this and would appreciate you coming forward now, rather than us finding out later after the internal investigation. At that point, we'll be unable to help you. If you have any information that will help us help your friend, please do come forward. We will appreciate the help, and your loyalty will be noted.

Your employees have now been told that you are on their side, fighting for them against the management, and that you are trying to save them. You are asking for their help and are telling them that you won't be able to help them if the issue isn't resolved before the investigation report is out and the upper management steps in. Automatically, the employees see you as a kindred soul who is trying to help them not "get" them. And to top it off, you have also said that you are going to look kindly upon any of the employees who help their friend by coming forward. You have told them that coming forward doesn't just have benefits for you, you're actually helping your friend instead of being a traitor.

How much more likely do you think it is that employees will come forward now?

Achievement unlocked!

Step Four: Share Concerns

Another important step to be observed if we want to encourage honest and open conversations is the identification of all the reasons that we don't want to talk about our problems. This has a particular upside to it as well, the more you talk about the concerns you have, like being laughed at, or not being understood, the less likely it is that they will come to fruition. This is because people are likely to do the opposite of what you tell them they will. If you are afraid the conversation you wish to have will be poorly received, tell them that. The odds are they will now make a conscious effort not to take it poorly, and your honesty is being translated to encourage them to also speak up—how perfect is that?

Step Five: Opinions vs. Facts

The next step? Being able to honestly differentiate between what you are imagining and what you are actually dealing with. When we deal with a situation, two things are happening simultaneously. On the one hand, you are taking in the facts of the matter, so you are noticing the actual happenings that are taking place, and on the other hand, you are dealing with your brain going haywire and converting these facts into possibilities by using your imagination. This means all the things that are happening are now morphing into a whole different issue based on where your imagination is taking you.

Why don't we break this down with an example to make things easier?

A dinner table conversation is taking place between your Republican brother, Donny, your Democratic sister, Hilary, and yourself. You happen to be an Independent in this particular context.

Donny: The Democrats just waste money on stupid

things like art and museums. No wonder they keep losing.

Hilary: Well, at least we aren't leeching money from the NRA and refusing to do anything about school children dying on a regular basis because we don't want to hurt our pockets.

You: Well, be that as it may, Donny does have a point. The Democrats do need to structure their fiscal plans better. Art and museums can wait, but our social security really can't.

Hilary: Are you going to vote Republican then? Don't you see that they are ruining the country with their supremacist ideals?

This is the problem with the way that Hilary has perceived your answer. She has assumed that because you agreed with Donny on one issue, you are now a Republican supporter who will vote Republican and are therefore anti-Democrat. She has also assumed that because you are a Republican you also support all of the other Republican propaganda including racial discrimination and white supremacy.

Hilary's imagination took over. The problem is now that her imagination is in the game. She's no longer focused on the facts—the fact being that you agreed that the

Democrats need to have better fiscal plans. She assumed that your agreement on one topic leads to your agreement on a bunch of other issues and that all of this now means that you are supporting the Republican Party, and she reacted based on that assumption.

In truth, all you said was that you agreed that the Democrats needed better financial planning. Period. No ifs, buts, or maybes.

Learn to take things at face value. If you don't, you'll find yourself acting like Hillary and reacting to a problem that doesn't exist.

Step Six: Make Requests

Now having problems is normal—but what you do about them is what really matters. If you have a problem with your boss or with management, instead of going around complaining about it and criticizing the system, why not come up with a solution and try to implement it?

If the problem is a lack of feedback, go to your supervisor and ask them to allocate an hour out of their schedule every week to give you feedback so that you can learn and understand your mistakes. Ask for the help you need. People aren't going to know what you want from some mystical crystal ball. You need to speak up and be proactive. It's ultimately all about whether or not you come up with a solution instead of constant complaints and problems so that the conversation moves forward.

Step Seven: The Benefit Analysis

The next question you need to ask because frankly, everyone else is asking it, is what is in it for the other guy? Whenever we want to communicate something, it's usually because we have some sort of vested interest in the issue, or in other words, we benefit from it. But us benefiting from it doesn't sort out the person on the other end of the communication. If you want them to be encouraged to speak and communicate with you, you have to offer them some sort of benefit—something that helps them out, or at the least motivates them.

Step Eight: The Follow up Plan

Once you have all that in place and have had that perfect open conversation you were looking for, what do you think your next step is going to be? Pina Coladas on a beach in New Mexico? No! Of course not. None of what you just did is worth anything if you didn't walk away from that conversation with a concrete plan! That is your follow-up plan. You need to have actions planned out which will help you implement everything you had going (kind of like what you've been getting at the end of every chapter!)

Step Nine: Appreciate *Everything*!

Honest, open communication is great and all but let's not lie and say that it's easy. Let's face it; it's anything but. Unfortunately, many people never do this again no matter how beneficial it is because they don't feel like the effort and the stress they had to execute the honest communication was appreciated.

Remember positive reinforcement is key! So, get out there and appreciate it!

To-Do Drills—Your OFFICIAL Action Items

Finally, it's drill time again. Now that you have a clear idea of what honest communication is and how you need to practice certain things to ensure you have a more effective conversation, it's time to put all of that to work. This time, we'll just give you a to-do list, and it's up to you to use the nine steps above like a checklist and implement it in every one of the given instances like the managers from the example. Ready?

1. Have an honest conversation with your significant other about problems you face regarding the relationship.

2. Have a conversation with your friend about a time when you were extremely hurt by a statement they made.

3. Have a conversation with your boss negotiating a pay rise.

4. Have a conversation with someone with an opposing viewpoint online without breaking out of the methods of communication you've been taught.

5. Have a conversation with yourself about what you feel

146

you need to do to move forward.

Come on now, don't be lazy. Get to work!

It may be daunting, but the only way out is through!

Chapter Five: How to Establish a Win-Win Scenario

"Win-win is a belief in the Third Alternative. It's not your way or my way; it's a better way, a higher way."—Stephen Covey

The last thing that we find ourselves dealing with as we wrap up the basics of effective communication is how to walk away from the table feeling like we've had fun, and how to ensure the same feeling for our opponent.

First off, don't think of the other person as your opponent. To truly be able to set up effective communication channels we need to be able to think of our audience in a positive manner, which basically isn't the case if you are calling them your opponents. If you're doing that, you're gearing up for a fight.

So, we're coming to the final issue—the crafting of a win-win scenario by bolstering effective communication. Now we've talked a lot about how to go about ensuring effective communication, and how it's important, but we never got around to talking about *why* we want to promote effective communication.

Take a minute and think about what the core objective of any form of communication is. Generally, it's to share ideas and to strike a balance in our relationships, or more specifically, to negotiate. Now think back to the last fight you had with your significant other. Did that feel like you were trying to negotiate something or did it feel like you were smashing your head open as both parties began to attack, label, or attempt to control each other's actions?

But that is just one end of the spectrum. Yelling and fighting is one way of trying to get your message across. The other is passive acquiescence where as opposed to fighting in an attempt to get your message across you just kind of make puppy eyes and hope that your audience or the person you are speaking to gets the message and doesn't try to railroad you.

Neither of those two methods are particularly delightful. Rather, the methods are both equally ineffective. So, what is the "right" way to deal with things? How do we engage and communicate our thoughts, without it turning into an all-out war zone?

In steps—Assertive communication.

Assertive communication is basically the communication that we have been teaching you about. Assertive communicators are honest, empathetic, and they take the time to listen while also ensuring that they are heard.

Assertive communication is the only form of communication that allows individuals to work together to identify key needs in both parties and to proactively work to address those needs in a manner which is mutually beneficial. Therefore, it allows both parties to leave the table satisfied and more importantly willing to engage again.

Which is precisely why we are now going to walk you through how to use all of these fancy techniques we've just taught you to craft your assertive approach to communication.

What do you think? Are you ready to finish your final task before you can become a master communicator?

Don't worry!

You've got this!

Here we go!

What Does Winning Feel Like?

Before we go off to list all the things that you need to do to ensure you feel like you have won something from a communication. Why don't we first try to identify the feeling of winning and what winning itself feels like.

Even though as a child the word winning seemed to denote some level of competition against peers or others, for most people as you grow up, the term "winning" becomes interchangeable with the word "success." It's not that you feel the intense need to be *numero uno* in an art competition. It's more that you have a goal you have set for yourself, and you want to attain it.

Pretty simple, isn't it?

Winning is a sense of accomplishment.

Okay, but now think of this. Is any form of accomplishment going to be something you feel good about? What if you achieved your task but had to make sacrifices you weren't comfortable with, or if you won in the end, but ugly things were said and they stayed with you? What if you won, but felt demeaned? Would that still be okay?

We'll go out on a limb and state that none of these forms of winning felt good or felt like a positive thing. Do you know what that means?

It means it wasn't winning.

The most important thing about winning is that when you are winning you walk away feeling better about yourself than you did before, and that is not going to happen if you weren't doing it right.

Also, keep in mind that all this time we've been talking about how *you* feel and how *you* are affected.

But in the end, effective communication doesn't base itself on *you*. It's based on both sides, which means both sides of the conversation need to feel good about themselves as they leave the table. This is going to take a little bit of maneuvering and a little bit of good planning. We'll start with the planning—sound good?

Planning for a Mutual Win

Now, since we are focusing on effective communication which can only occur when two parties are present and pleased with the outcome of a conversation, we are going to find a way to start planning mutual successes.

But, how does one do that?

Where do you begin?

Ideally, you will start with the challenges. Obviously, you and the person you are communicating information to aren't necessarily on the same page with everything. This is where the conflict comes in and subsequently where the challenge arises. Your job now is to find and identify these differences to find a way around them. That's Step One: *Recognition*.

Once you've found and acknowledged the differences you need to move on and find something you can both agree on so you can pour in a bit of positive reinforcement, or simply just say, "Yes, I totally agree."That is Step Two: *Establishing Common Ground*.

If you have been able to complete both of these steps satisfactorily, you have now set the stage for open conversation. It's now time for you to respectfully start to engage in detailed conversation in regard to the different opinions and try to find a mutually beneficial way to overcome the differences in opinion you have. This is a combination of three steps **Establishing Respect, Balanced Overtures,** and finally, the **Development of a Mutually Beneficial Plan of Action.**

Sounds just about perfect doesn't it—but hold on! Before we jump the gun and start working on this winning master plan, we need to make sure that we have the perfect way to utilize it. We need to have a clear **Follow Up** that will help us deal with the aftermath.

Now we're ready!

And for the last time, here we go!

Step One: Recognition

Any form of communication needs a base, and the base of any effective communication needs to be a recognition and acknowledgment of the issues at hand. The issues at hand being the differences we each have and our right to have those mutually exclusive opinions and how they impact our minds, our thoughts, and our future plans.

What we're getting at here is that both parties need to be heard out.

This can be difficult, particularly because active listening is not something we are used to doing. Even if we are trying to hear what the other party has to say if when we try to explain ourselves and our point of view the other party isn't being equally responsive, it can feel extremely aggravating.

Let's put it into context, shall we?

You are a wealthy white Republican voter, named Harold from uptown New York. You are understanding of the concept of racial disparity but don't feel politically motivated issues should have an impact on academics as the United States is a country with free primary and secondary education. You are debating the issue "affirmative action" or to be more explicit the matter of "quotas" for black or minority students in IVY League universities, one of which is your alumnus. Your son, Harold is the same age as the person you are speaking with, a prospective Harvard alumnus by the name William who was admitted via affirmative action.

The conversation goes as follows.

Harold: Affirmative action makes no sense to me, and I really think it should be banned. There were plenty of black students at Harvard in my time, and there are even more now. The system is unfair and makes no sense. Students should get to go to top universities based on their scores and merit, not because of their skin color.

William: While I agree that merit should be the basis of selection, I feel like you are missing the point of affirmative action which is that scores only count where there is an even base to start from. Most black children are not raised with the same privileges as white children, and as such, without affirmative action barely stand a chance.

Harold: That's nonsense. Are you sure it's not just because you don't want to work hard for it? Because that's what it seems like to me.

William: Why is it nonsense, because it doesn't fit in with your narrative? It seems to me that you're just racist and want white people to get all the good stuff.

Okay, now, what do you think the problem with this conversation was?

Initially, the first two lines seemed fine/ Harold said what he thought, and then William made his point. So what went wrong?

Well, you'll notice that Harold's second line clearly shows that while William was listening to his concerns and responding respectfully, Harold was not interested in what he had to say, and instead brushed off his concerns and demeaned him at the same time. This showed William that not only did he have little regard for his thoughts he also had little regard for him as a person.

This disrespect coupled with his obvious unwillingness to listen, quickly resulted in William's own attitude towards the whole situation changing. You'll notice that in his next response when William realizes that his opinion will not be respected, he too ceases to be respectful and instead becomes confrontational. The entire conversation leads to no productive result, and no one wins.

Now, look at this scenario where two romantic partners are discussing an issue which they disagree on regarding their son, Jiyong.

Parent 1: I don't think Jiyong should stay in school. He's been getting bullied a lot recently, and I think homeschooling is the best option for him.

Parent 2: I understand, but I have a different opinion. While he has been bullied, it's been getting better, and he is starting to actually make friends there. Don't you think homeschooling would isolate him?

Parent 1: Do you think he'll be isolated? I actually never thought of that. I just wanted to get him out of the proximity of those bullies since I feel like it's going to affect his psyche as he grows up. I also haven't really seen him with any friends even though he's said he has made them. Do you think we should talk to him about it?

Parent 2: I do. I still think that facing adversity and getting through it is a better way to deal with the whole issue, but if you think that homeschooling is a better option, I would prefer putting it to him and seeing what he has to say. What do you think?

Parent 1: I agree. Let's talk to him before making any concrete decisions. Thanks, Babe.

Notice that in this conversation both parties have elected to see and acknowledge the differences in opinion. In fact, not only have they chosen to see and recognize their differences, but they have also made it a point to accept the points being made by the opposing parties. Clear communication has occurred which is exactly what we were going for.

Step Two: Establishing Common Ground

The next thing you need to do is find out a way to agree on something. This is critical because it is hard to have a conversation, particularly a difficult conversation if you don't agree on anything. This is a critical part of advancing mutual interests and cannot be done without. You'll find that the more difficult a topic is, or the more conflicting the viewpoints are, the more crucial it is that you find common ground, as, without it, you'll find it hard to agree on anything at all.

Let's take a look at a sample scenario:

You and your best friend have been discussing the inflammatory response that the Queensland Senator, Fraser Anning had to the terrorist attack conducted by a white Australian on a mosque in Christchurch, New Zealand. Your friend, Eric believes that Anning, despite having a crass way of putting it had a valid point, while you believe that Anning had no business making the statement he did, as a human being, much less as a political figure.

The conversation is as follows.

You: Senator Anning is a disgrace to Australia and the

world. I don't understand how a public figure like him could openly encourage the mass murder and terrorism that took place in Christchurch. He doesn't deserve to be in office.

Eric: Be that as it may, and I do agree he shouldn't have been publicly endorsing a terrorist act, he isn't alone in his point of view. There are plenty of other politicians and people in general who think like him.

You: What do you mean?

Eric: Immigration is a hot topic nowadays, and Fraser's claim has some merit. There are terrorists immigrating here from other countries and bombing our own people. It's not surprising that some extremist would try to get back in the same manner, right?

You: I think I see where you're going with this, and while I can understand what you're saying about retaliation, I think what you're missing out on is the fact that not all acts of terrorism come from outside sources. The problem isn't with the immigration. It's with the lack of integration, which is why Christchurch happened. The whole concept of us versus them is what's causing it.

Eric: Well yes, somewhat, but the problem wouldn't really be this prominent if people weren't immigrating in as much, don't you think?

Notice that both of you have very different takes on how valid Senator Anning's response is, and yet you have been able to continue to communicate clearly and without degrading each other because you are agreeing on one or two fundamental issues, like the fact that the reaction Anning had was inappropriate in the given circumstances.

Step Three: Establishing Respect

Another important part of communication is respect. You aren't going to get anywhere with people if you are continually demeaning them or treating them as if they don't matter. Which is exactly why it's so important to make sure that you respect other people. Now, the key issue here is dogmatism, and we've talked about dogmatism before, but we haven't really seen it in action.

Dogmatism is when someone chooses to believe that they are the only person who is right and when they are standing true in their idea without regard for any other person. The problem with this kind of behavior is that you can't expect someone else to respect you when you are not respectful yourself.

If you want someone to be kind and to listen to you as you explain your point, you need to afford them the same respect and do the same for them. Remember, do unto others as you would have them do unto you. A great way to make sure you are respectful is by cutting negative words out of your vocabulary. Instead of saying things like "I don't think that's going to happen," or "No, I don't want that," try to frame the sentences more positively, like "Wow, that sounds really great, but I think it may be a little difficult to get higher management to agree," or "Honestly, although I can see where you're coming from I'm not sure that is how I envisioned this project." Remember, regardless of what people may say, brute honestly is not cool or more effective it doesn't make you more intelligent or a better communicator. All it does is make you a bully.

Is honesty important? Yes! Of course, it is.

But so is respect and if your approach to honesty is overshadowing or destroying your respectfulness to another party, you really need to find a different way.

As Facebook COO Sheryl Sandberg put it, "Communication works best when we combine appropriateness with authenticity, finding that sweet spot where opinions are not brutally honest but delicately honest."

Step Four: Balancing Overtures

Balanced overtures refer to a sense of equity that is crucial to any form of communication, but particularly business communication where you are seeking to make an effective decision. Think about it like this. If you are having a conversation with someone, and they are constantly pushing you to make a decision. Even if it is the right decision, you aren't going to walk away from that conversation feeling fulfilled much less like you want to have a conversation with them again at some point.

At the same time, if you are the one pushing and forcing an opinion on someone, you can't expect them to feel like they are getting a good deal. The only thing they are going to be thinking of is when they can get out of there.

Think about this in the context of a sexual relationship between a man and a woman. The man, Jordan, is unwilling to have sexual intercourse as he feels strongly that sex is meant to be shared only between married couples. His girlfriend, Ivanka, laughs off these claims and insists on having sex in their relationship, as she thinks it's normal. Their conversation is as follows:

Jordan: I don't think I'm ready for this. In fact, I'm not

sure I want to do this at all before I'm married.

Ivanka: (laughing) Don't be silly, Jordan, it's not like it hurts the first time for men. Besides, I'm on my pill.

Jordan: I'm really not comfortable with the idea though. I'd feel guilty afterward.

Ivanka: You know you're basically telling me you don't want me. Do you really not feel anything for me? Come on; you know you do. It'll feel so good as well.

Jordan: I'd feel bad about it later, and it's not about you.

Ivanka: If you don't agree, I think we're going to have to break up. You don't want to break up, do you?

In this scenario, Ivanka consciously evades all of Jordan's objections and keeps pushing what she wants as if the only thing that matters is her consent. As a result, even if Jordan agrees to have sex, he's only doing so because he is being bullied into it, and that leads Jordan to feel devalued and objectified as a person. In the long run, the constant tendency to overpower Jordan's consent is going to lead to one-way communication between the two which is fatal to any relationship.

This is why there needs to be an element of balance between both parties during any form of communication. A deal where only one party wins is never a good deal because it effectively closes the door on future communication from that particular source resulting in a dead end when a new problem arises.

Long story short—don't just focus on the immediate result. Short-term wins will mean nothing if you are ruining the relationship, entirely. Your short-term wins need to build up to a bigger win not break off and scatter.

Step Five: Developing a Mutually Beneficial Plan

The best way to communicate effectively is to do so in a manner where there are benefits and compromises on both sides. A great way to encourage this in your opponent is by first creating a clear list of the things you are willing to negotiate on and another list of the things you require absolutely. Have your audience or the opposite party do the same, then have a clear discussion based on the given points.

Start with one of the things you can negotiate on and as a gesture of good faith, give in. This doesn't mean you should always give in to maintain peace, or that you should ever give in on a topic you feel strongly about. Any concessions you make should come from your negotiable items list and is merely meant to be a token gesture to show your opponent that you are willing to go the extra mile and that they too need to be able to step up. Not only does this give your opponent a positive impression of you and your motives, but it makes them more likely to try to emulate you and also be considerate during negotiations.

Let's look at this in the context of a business deal, where Party A is looking to purchase three apartments from Party B. The communication goes as follows:

Party A: While we really love all three apartments, we don't think six million is an appropriate evaluation for all three, and don't feel comfortable with that price for apartment 2 in particular as it is almost half the size of apartment 3.

Party B: Thank you! We're glad that you like them. Are you comfortable with the evaluations on the other ones?

Party A: Well, yes, and no. Apartment 1 has a beautiful view and is well worth the two million asking price, but apartment 3 while being much more spacious, doesn't really have a great view and can't be modified in any way either due to the building restraints, so we feel that one should have a lower price as well.

Party B: Hmm, that's unfortunate. With apartment 2, we are actually entertaining higher offers but are willing to drop down to 1.8 million dollars if you are taking all three. With apartment 3 however, we aren't able to do anything in terms of the pricing as the costing is too high. However, we can speak to the public authorities for you and see if we can get you renovation permission. The renovation would have to be at your own cost, however.

Party A: So, you can't do anything about apartment 3 at all?

Party B: No, unfortunately not.

Party A: Well, to be honest, the discounted price on apartment 2 makes up for the issue a bit, and the renovation would be the cherry on top. So if the permission works out, it's a yes from us.

Party B: Perfect! How about we get back to you as soon as we hear back from the planning authorities?

Party A: We'll look forward to it.

In the given example both parties choose to acknowledge and accept the concessions made by the other parties, and without pushing or being overbearing in any way. That is to say, without using threats or manipulation to found a mutually beneficial plan.

This is the perfect example of how a mutually beneficial plan is a great way to ensure that your communication is effective and productive, with both of the parties feeling like they have achieved something. The best thing is if mutual issues are heard out properly even if you can't come to a joint decision, you still don't feel drained or unhappy which leaves the door open for possible future interactions. Which is exactly how you want things to be.

No deal is better than a forced deal because once you force something, you are ruining a channel of communication forever, and we don't want that, do we?

Step Six: Following Up

And that brings us to the final step in this journey.

Following up.

Having a good effective plan that you have developed after having a great honest and respectful conversation with your opponent is a perfect way to implement your new-found communication skills. However, none of these skills are worth anything if you aren't following them up with a strict action plan.

Be clear and concise, yes, but also be effective!

Conclusion

"To effectively communicate, we must realize that we are all different in the way we perceive the world and use this understanding as a guide to our communications with others."—Tony Robbins

And that brings us to the end—it's been a pretty long journey, hasn't it?

To start with, let us take a moment to thank you for buying Effective Communication: 5 Essential Tips and Exercises to Improve How You Communicate in This Divided World, Even If It Is About Politics, Race or Gender! We sincerely hope that the book has been able to help you effectively and systematically form a better understanding of the best methods and techniques to develop an effective communication style.

With the world being more divided now than it ever was before, the immediate impact on our personal and professional lives is a key source of stress for almost all of us. While most individuals may flounder or struggle to understand how to deal with this, you've just proved your mettle by taking the first step to face this issue head-on.

But as we've said before, this book is merely a guide. In fact, why don't you think of it as a road map?

As a communicator, you need to figure out what works best for you and the interests that you represent. Use the techniques you've been offered but do not feel compelled to be ruled by them. Remember, being yourself is the most important thing!

Which is why on that final note, we want to remind you that it is super important to us that you know your trust in us to provide you with a quality read is something we treasure! We are grateful for your support, and we can only hope that you feel that we have delivered on our promise. If so, please do leave a review! We'd love to hear from you!

100 % FREE Ebook!

LEARN HOW YOU CAN ENJOY YOUR GADGETS WITHOUT LOSING YOUR ABILITY TO COMMUNICATE IN REAL LIFE!

Claim Your Free Copy Now!

https://maxjharrison.com/moderntechnology

References

3 Golden Rules For Honest Communication. (2015). Retrieved April 6, 2019, from Mind Movies Blog website: https://www.mindmovies.com/blogroll/3-golden-rules-for-honest-communication

5 Tips for Building Effective Delivery Skills - Business Communications. (2011, March 31). Retrieved April 6, 2019, from Business Communications website: https://managementhelp.org/blogs/communications/2011/03/09/5-tips-for-building-effective-delivery-skills/

Ahmed, S. (2016a). An Evaluation of Effective Communication Skills Coursebook. *Advances in Language and Literary Studies*, 7(3), 57–70. Retrieved from http://www.journals.aiac.org.au/index.php/alls/article/view/2264/1985

Ahmed, S. (2016b). An Evaluation of Effective Communication Skills Coursebook. *Advances in Language and Literary Studies*, 7(3), 57–70. Retrieved from https://doaj.org/article/d0af18481f134a149a9eee2efcb90faa

Amy Rees Anderson. (2015, May 15). Good Employees Make Mistakes. Great Leaders Allow Them To. *Forbes*. Retrieved from https://www.forbes.com/sites/amyanderson/2013/04/17/good-employees-make-mistakes-great-leaders-allow-them-to/#44b74b0a126a

Baker, J. (2018, April 23). PeopleResults. Retrieved April 6, 2019, from PeopleResults website: https://www.people-results.com/call-empathy-key-effective-communication-relationships/

Be Honest: Are You Communicating Effectively? |. (2017, September 12). Retrieved April 6, 2019, from Beyondphilosophy.com website: https://beyondphilosophy.com/honest-communicating-effectively/

Beyond dogmatism: 6 ways to move towards understanding. (2017, December 19). Retrieved April 6, 2019, from AgileUprising website: http://agileuprising.com/2017/12/19/beyond-dogmatism-6-ways-to-move-towards-understanding/

Building Trust Through Honesty and Open Communication. (2012, July 30). Retrieved April 6, 2019, from Makarios Consulting website: http://makariosconsulting.com/building-trust-through-honesty-and-open-communication/

Chapter 13 COMMUNICATION INTRODUCTION. (n.d.). Retrieved from https://www.faa.gov/about/initiatives/maintenance_h f/library/documents/media/human_factors_maintena nce/human_factors_guide_for_aviation_maintenance _-_chapter_13.communication.pdf

comfreaksolution.com. (2019a). The Winning Tools for Effective Communication - Focus Learning Consulting Sdn Bhd. Retrieved April 6, 2019, from Focus Learning Consulting Sdn Bhd website: http://www.focuslearning.com.my/services/training/w tfc/

comfreaksolution.com. (2019b). The Winning Tools for Effective Communication - Focus Learning Consulting Sdn Bhd. Retrieved from Focus Learning Consulting Sdn Bhd website: http://www.focuslearning.com.my/services/training/w tfc/

Communicating With Integrity Helps Organizations Endure Change. (2017, October 26). Retrieved April 6, 2019, from PRSA website: http://apps.prsa.org/Intelligence/TheStrategist/Article s/view/12077/1149/Communicating_With_Integrity_ Helps_Organizations_E#.XKjxABMzaRs

Communication: Let's Be Honest. (2015, June 9).

Retrieved April 6, 2019, from Makarios Consulting website: http://makariosconsulting.com/communication-lets-honest/

Crews, N. E. (1979). Developing empathy for effective communication. *AORN Journal*, *30*(3), 536–548. https://doi.org/10.1016/s0001-2092(07)62963-9

Edinger, S. (2013, March 21). If You Want to Communicate Better, Read This. *Forbes*. Retrieved from https://www.forbes.com/sites/scottedinger/2013/03/20/if-you-want-to-communicate-better-read-this/#b9602722dd1a

Effects of Negative Communication in the Workplace. (2019). Retrieved April 6, 2019, from Chron.com website: https://smallbusiness.chron.com/effects-negative-communication-workplace-11524.html

Emotional Intelligence (EQ) | The Premier Provider - Tests, Training, Certification, and Coaching. - TalentSmart. (2018). Retrieved April 6, 2019, from TalentSmart website: http://www.talentsmart.com/articles/How-Complaining-Rewires-Your-Brain-for-Negativity-2147446676-p-1.html

Fisher, E. (2018, April 13). Integrity in Communication:

Prove it with Action - AdLibbing.org. Retrieved April 6, 2019, from AdLibbing.org website: https://www.adlibbing.org/2018/04/13/integrity-in-communication-prove-it-with-action/

Honest Communication. (2019). Retrieved April 6, 2019, from Learningtogive.org website: https://www.learningtogive.org/units/character-education-honesty-grade-8/honest-communication

Honesty Is the Best Policy: Effective communication is essential for achieving a good death. (2008, December 30). Retrieved from MD Magazine website: https://www.mdmag.com/journals/oncng-oncologynursing/2008/oncnurse_december_2008/ho nesty_best_policy

How to Love People: The Heart of Effective Communication. (2015a, March 28). Retrieved April 6, 2019, from TowerOfPower.com.au website: https://www.towerofpower.com.au/the-heart-of-effective-communication-how-to-love-people

How to Love People: The Heart of Effective Communication. (2015b, March 28). Retrieved from TowerOfPower.com.au website: https://www.towerofpower.com.au/the-heart-of-effective-communication-how-to-love-people

https://www.facebook.com/communicationtraining. (2018a, June 8). Silent Treatment: How to handle it-- Effective Communication Skills Training. Retrieved April 6, 2019, from Dan OConnor Training website: https://www.danoconnortraining.com/silent-treatment-handling/

https://www.facebook.com/communicationtraining. (2018b, June 8). Silent Treatment: How to handle it-- Effective Communication Skills Training. Retrieved from Dan OConnor Training website: https://www.danoconnortraining.com/silent-treatment-handling/

https://www.facebook.com/OrnaAndMatthew. (2014, January 29). The Thin Line Between Brutal Honesty And Authentic Communication. Retrieved April 6, 2019, from YourTango website: https://www.yourtango.com/experts/orna-and-matthew-walters/honesty-really-best-policy

KELLERMANN, K. (1989). The Negativity Effect in Interaction It's All in Your Point of View. *Human Communication Research*, *16*(2), 147–183. https://doi.org/10.1111/j.1468-2958.1989.tb00208.x

Melissa. (2013, January 11). How Negative Language Hinders Your Communication – Effective Communication | Expert Advice. Retrieved April 6,

2019, from Effectivecommunicationadvice.com website: http://effectivecommunicationadvice.com/negative-language

PowerofPositivity. (2017, June 12). Psychologists Explain How To Stop Gossip Immediately. Retrieved April 6, 2019, from Power of Positivity: Positive Thinking & Attitude website: https://www.powerofpositivity.com/psychologists-reveal-the-one-phrase-to-stop-gossiping-immediately-still-in-progress/

Rodger Dean Duncan. (2014, November 8). Excuses, Excuses: Leadership That Avoids The Blame Game. *Forbes*. Retrieved from https://www.forbes.com/sites/rodgerdeanduncan/2014/11/08/excuses-excuses-leadership-that-avoids-the-blame-game/#4b27bbe63c2a

Roy, A. (2018, June 12). Avelo Roy. Retrieved April 6, 2019, from Avelo Roy website: https://aveloroy.com/2015/04/18/effectively-communicate-win-over-irrational-people/

Stillman, J. (2016, February 29). Complaining Is Terrible for You, According to Science. Retrieved April 6, 2019, from Inc.com website: https://www.inc.com/jessica-stillman/complaining-rewires-your-brain-for-negativity-science-says.html

Three Simple Statements That Cure Dogmatism and Open Minds. (2015). Retrieved April 6, 2019, from Psychology Today website: https://www.psychologytoday.com/us/blog/brainsnacks/201512/three-simple-statements-cure-dogmatism-and-open-minds

to. (2018). 7 C's of Effective communication. Retrieved from https://www.youtube.com/watch?v=7JZ1v-VwTXg

What is Integrity-Based Communications (IBC)? (2014). Retrieved April 6, 2019, from Linkedin.com website: https://www.linkedin.com/pulse/20141117232256-5989008-what-is-integrity-based-communications-ibc/

White, K. (2006). *Effective Communication Independent Study.* Retrieved from https://training.fema.gov/emiweb/downloads/is242.pdf

(2019). Retrieved April 6, 2019, from Lifehacker.com website: https://lifehacker.com/use-the-hail-method-to-be-more-persuasive-and-trustwort-1599169164

www.ingramcontent.com/pod-product-compliance
Lightning Source LLC
Chambersburg PA
CBHW020909180526
45163CB00007B/2681